NIETZSCHE, PROPHET OF NAZISM: THE CULT OF THE SUPERMAN

Unveiling the Nazi Secret Doctrine

by
ABIR TAHA

authorHOUSE™

1663 LIBERTY DRIVE, SUITE 200
BLOOMINGTON, INDIANA 47403
(800) 839-8640
WWW.AUTHORHOUSE.COM

First published by AuthorHouse 05/23/05

ISBN: 1-4208-4121-1 (sc)

Printed in the United States of America
Bloomington, Indiana

This book is printed on acid-free paper.

"Not 'mankind' but Superman is the goal!"

Friedrich Nietzsche

PREFACE

The "Cult of the Superman" has haunted humanity throughout history, yet it was only clearly expressed in the philosophy of its modern prophet, Friedrich Nietzsche, and culminated in its fiercest supporter, the National Socialist ideology, a political religion whose main ideal and objective were the creation of a superhuman species.

By showing the link between the Nietzschean and Nazi worldviews - and more specifically the Nazi Secret Doctrine which I have called "esoteric Nazism"- my aim is to demonstrate that the Nazis were pure Nietzscheans, thus repudiating the views of some scholars who deny or undermine any link between the Nietzschean and Nazi doctrines. I endeavour to prove that the Nazi esoteric ideology was primarily an endeavour to actualise and institutionalise Nietzsche's cult of the Superman, applying it to a political system that would breed a *Herrenvolk* or "Master Race" in body and spirit, destined to rule the earth. Nazism was in fact greatly influenced by Nietzsche's philosophy, especially his concept of the Superman, giving it a political dimension in order to "put Nietzsche into motion" and turn the philosopher's cult from an abstract notion into a concrete reality. The S.S. (*Schutzstaffeln*, or "Security Squads"), Nazi Germany's racial and political elite, was indeed a self-proclaimed Nietzschean institution of *Übermenschen* or "Supermen" claiming to embody the creed of the Godlike man.

Thus did both Nietzsche and the Nazis call for a revival of Aryan paganism, namely the ancient Aryan esoteric tradition from India to Greece, rejecting the Jewish religion of Christianity, which they believed was a gross distortion of Christ's original teachings. Both doctrines acknowledged the Will to Power as the motor of history; both praised the qualities and values of the Superman, glorifying war, and advocating a radically aristocratic view of the world. Both Nietzsche and Nazism despised Western Judaeo-Christian Civilisation and its two products, Liberalism and Socialism, introducing a "third option" - aristocratic radicalism - between "corrupt egalitarian democracy" and the "materialist socialism of the mob". In addition, both advocated the rule of an Aryan universal "Master Race" transcending the boundaries of states and nations; and finally, both Nietzsche and the Nazis dismissed the "decadent" Jew from civilisation, considering him alien to the natural order, an incarnation of the slave morality.

TABLE OF CONTENTS

INTRODUCTION

From times immemorial, mankind has been fascinated by a myth, a great yet impossible dream: the creation of the perfect man, the Superman, direct descendant of the ancient gods. Hence, throughout history, a veritable "Cult of the Superman" has been haunting the imagination of philosophers and rulers alike, yet this cult remained a vague and unrealistic fantasy until it was clearly formulated in a coherent philosophy by Friedrich Nietzsche (1844-1900), the modern prophet of the Superman. Nonetheless, it wasn't until the advent of National Socialism, its staunchest supporter, that this cult reached its climax and moved from theory to practice, being transformed by the Nazis into a political ideology aimed at breeding a Master Race fit for world rule.

It was thus only natural for Nazism to be profoundly influenced by Nietzsche's philosophy, since this doctrine shared so many values with the German philosopher, who was best known for his preaching of the rule of the Superman, his veneration of force, his advocacy of power politics and his aristocratic contempt for egalitarian and "weak" doctrines such as Judaeo-Christianity, Liberal Democracy and Socialism. Indeed, the Nazis were "tough Nietzscheans", and their racial Aristocracy, the S.S. (*Schutzstaffeln* or "Security Squads"), was a self-styled Nietzschean institution of Supermen claiming to embody the values and virtues of the godlike man. The extent of Nietzsche's influence on Nazism has in fact prompted writers such as H.F. Peters to say that *"no modern thinker, with the exception of Karl Marx, has had such a fateful influence on the course of world history" (1)*.

Before going further in our investigation, however, one might ask, why is it still significant, now that perfectionist theories (and Nazism at their head) are altogether rejected and condemned as "biased", "politically incorrect", "undemocratic", or even "evil", to reveal the intimate connection existing between the Nazi doctrine and Nietzsche's thought, let alone study the concept of the Superman, which seems obsolete in a liberal world that has ruled out the teleological ideal of human perfection, embracing as ultimate reality and purpose the mere "will to live". i.e., self-preservation, as opposed to the Will to Power and self-overcoming?

The answer is that, although the idea of the existence of superior beings on earth infuriates the partisans of democracy and the advocates of equality among men, who ignore it, condemn it, or simply consider it a "myth", the concept of the Superman deserves a close study, for only by doing so would we be able to comprehend the significance of this noble cause and the profound impact it has had on modern world history. Indeed, this seemingly harmless idealistic cause has in fact led to the Second World War, the bloodiest and fiercest conflict of contemporary history, where thousands of *Totenkopf* ("Death's head") S.S. squads, believers in the millenarian Cult of the Superman, murdered without mercy all "sub-humans" whose existence impeded the evolution of humanity- and who were thus considered enemies of the "New Order"- and died unhesitatingly for the sake of producing a Higher humanity.

What's more, this cult from such a different, mysterious and mythical world, still fascinates, up to this day and in this radically egalitarian age, an elect few, who are bewildered by its adoration of force and energy, spirituality and perfection, and its exclusive, esoteric and incommunicable knowledge reserved only for the initiated elite. In the light of this, the present comparative study acquires a whole new meaning, for it enables us to penetrate deeper into the essence of two perfectionist doctrines (the Nietzschean and Nazi doctrines) deeply enshrined in a pre-Christian pagan spiritual tradition aimed at creating the God-man, a heritage which goes back to the origins of civilisation, at a time when humanity was guided by the teachings of the "Great Ones", i.e. spiritual Masters now considered legendary mythical figures by our positivist-materialistic civilisation which lacks a sense of purpose or a vision of the universe. Rama, Krishna, Manu, Zarathustra, Prometheus, Orpheus, Hermes, Pythagoras, Plato, … and finally, Jesus Christ, were all prototypes of the "Son of God", the God-man which the "Cult of the Superman" strives to re-create.

It is therefore of prime importance to study the Cult of the Superman and consequently to analyse the interconnection between its two fiercest advocates: Friedrich Nietzsche (1844-1900), the philosopher who wrote about the Superman, and Nazism, the political ideology which fought to create him. Although Nazism was a modern millenarian revolution based on the ancient esoteric tradition of Aryan Occultism, and would have emerged regardless of Nietzsche's prior existence (though maybe with a different look), it was nevertheless profoundly and directly influenced by Nietzsche's philosophy. The Nazis were in fact faithful disciples of Nietzsche, practising and advocating almost everything he preached] and typical Nietzschean tenets such as "Superman", "Master Race", "Will to Power", "Immoralism", "Transvaluation of Values", "Beyond Good and Evil",

"Master versus Slave Moralities", "War", "Domination", "Exploitation", "Breeding", ... became of very common use in Nazi literature.

The crucial task of this book is to show the striking similarities between Nietzsche's philosophy and National Socialism, through comparative and textual analysis of major works written on and by Nietzsche and the Nazis. This method of research will involve a critical approach towards selected passages of the cited sources in order to show the link between the two doctrines, by presenting valid and reliable evidence in support of my assumptions and determining the range of permissible inferences and interpretations. *acknowledges the assumptions*

In doing so, I will analyse and penetrate deep into the inner and real meaning of the Nazi doctrine, i.e. "Esoteric Nazism", in the light of Nietzsche's influence, showing that the Nazi doctrine had deep occult sources (Aryanism, Ariosophy, Armanism, Theosophy, Hermetism, Theo-Zoology, Neo-Templarism, Rosicrucianism, Wotanism), and relied on works of mystical and occult writers (H.S. Chamberlain, Richard Wagner, Meister Eckhart, Carl Gustav Jung, Aleister Crowley, George Gurdjieff, Dietrich Eckart, Karl Haushofer, Herbert Reichstein, Guido Von List, Lanz Von Liebenfels, Karl Maria Wiligut, Rudolf Von Sebottendorff, the Nazi scientist Hans Hoerbiger), in addition to the influence on Nazi ideology of Secret Societies (the Thule Gesellschaft, the Edda society, the Hermetic Order of the Golden Dawn, the Order of the New Templars, the Luminous Lodge or Vril Society, the Germanenorden)... These sources reveal the esoteric tradition in which this movement was deeply enshrined. Nietzsche was undoubtedly the direct and the major, but certainly not the only source of Nazi ideology; in fact, both theories belonged to the same pagan Aryanist-mystical tradition and to the perfectionist-elitist paradigm.

major & direct vew point of view

The contribution of this book is two-fold: it analyses Esoteric Nazism, whose spirit was best exemplified by the S.S., Nazi Germany's aristocracy, in contrast to the popular exoteric Nazi doctrine championed by the *Sturmabteilungen*, i.e. the "Storm Troopers", or S.A., and then establishes a link with Nietzsche's philosophy, demonstrating that the Nazi elite was truly Nietzschean.

The first chapter deals with the controversial Nietzsche-Nazi connection, establishing a clear link between Nietzsche's universal aristocratic thought and esoteric Nazism. The second chapter deals with the revival of Aryan paganism which Nietzsche and the Nazis were striving to achieve, as staunch neo-pagans advocating a return to the pre-Christian Aryan esoteric tradition from India to Greece. The Nazi cult was indeed a modern occult phenomenon that had inherited the millenarian Aryan pagan tradition. The neo-paganism professed by Nietzsche and the Nazis also contrasted the figure of Christ, whom both doctrines admired, with Judaeo-Christianity, which they despised as a distortion of Jesus' original teachings.

The third chapter deals with the concept of the Will to Power, a central theme in Nietzsche's philosophy, which the Nazis adopted as the main tenet of their ideology, and which, in my opinion, implies, first, a transvaluation of values; second, self-overcoming; and third, the overcoming of others. For Nietzsche and his disciples, the Nazis, the Will to Power was, first, the origin of morality: in this respect, Nietzsche's and the Nazis' rejection of transcendentalism, exemplified by the "death" of the transcendent God, or "active nihilism", constitutes man's great liberation and paves the ground for an immanentist morality "beyond Good and Evil" which would ultimately lead to the Superman as mankind's new and highest purpose. Hence, the "immoralism" professed by Nietzsche and the Nazis means a rejection of a universal morality for all, calling instead for a transvaluation of the values of "Good" and "Evil" (which means that everything that was hitherto named "good" should now be termed "bad", and vice-versa), i.e. a call for the rule of the values of the "Master Morality" of antiquity versus the actually prevailing "Slave Morality". Second, the Will to Power concept also implies self-overcoming, which is man's highest goal, the bridge to the Superman, according to both the Nietzschean and Nazi doctrines. Finally, the Will to Power concept represents the drive for conquest and domination. Indeed, both Nietzsche and the Nazis viewed war as higher life-affirmation and justified the domination, exploitation, and even the elimination of the weak multitude by the strong elite.

Further in my investigation of the Nietzsche-Nazi connection, the fourth chapter discusses the aristocratic worldview of Nietzsche and Nazism. It first explains how the "enemies of the Superman", namely Socialism and Liberalism, were despised by Nietzsche and the Nazis alike, for both considered that these egalitarian ideologies embodied the rule of the "Last Man", and could only produce modernity's mediocre "men without chests". The "aristocratic radicalism" advocated by Nietzsche and the Nazis, which was characterised by "spiritual racism", constituted a "third option" between 'corrupt egalitarian democracy' and the 'materialist socialism of the mob', and sought to apply Eugenics in order to breed an

Aryan universal Master Race transcending the political boundaries of Nation-states.

Nietzsche liked the Jews!

I then endeavour to prove, relying on selected passages of Nietzschean and Nazi literature, that they both professed a racist-aristocratic and spiritual brand of anti-Semitism, a deep and thorough hostility to, and contempt for, the Jewish Spirit which they believed was utterly despicable: the Jew was in fact the supreme decadent, the typical *Untermensch* ("subhuman"), the perfect antithesis to the Superman, for he embodied the slave morality to perfection and was hence behind all the decadent movements of history (Judaeo-Christianity, Socialism, Liberalism, Democracy…).

1933 is a significant date in world history, in more than one respect: this year not only witnessed the coming to power of the Nazi phenomenon, with its drastic implications on the course of world history; it was also the first historical attempt, by an organised political group, to apply Nietzsche's philosophy, especially his cult of the Superman, to a political system (it is worth noting in this respect that Nietzsche did not specify any mechanism for the breeding of the Superman), for the Nazis considered that they were answering Nietzsche's call for the "solitary Supermen" (in his famous *Thus Spoke Zarathustra*) to end their confinement, get organised and united as a Master Race which would rule over ordinary humanity.

CHAPTER ONE

NIETZSCHE AND ESOTERIC NAZISM

*intended for or likely
to be understood by only a
small number of people
with a specialized knowledge
or interest*

Nietzsche and the Nazis: a controversial relationship

The extent of Nietzsche's influence on Nazi ideology has been the object of a great debate among scholars: the problems of interpretation of the philosopher's writings have indeed stirred profound controversy over the Nietzsche-Nazi connection, and the debate has until this day not been resolved, the Nietzsche scholars still being divided into three main categories or approaches: first, those who view Nietzsche as a 'Nazi'; second, those who view him as partly a Nazi; and third, those who view Nietzsche as anti-Nazi. Each category of scholars presents a different interpretation of the philosopher's writings, and hence establishes or denies a link with Nazism.

The first category of scholars view Nietzsche as an apologist for Nazism, due to his anti-Christian, radically racist and aristocratic philosophy which preached the coming of the Superman and praised war and the subjugation of lower races by the Master Race. The Nazi scholar Alfred Bauemler; Nietzsche's sister, Elisabeth Foerster-Nietzsche; the pro-Nazi scholar Anthony Ludovici, who all translated or edited several of Nietzsche's books, fall into this category, which also includes Georg Luckacs, the Marxist scholar who saw a definite link between the Nietzschean and Nazi doctrines; and the Nazi scholar H. Haertle, who pinpointed what of Nietzsche a "good Nazi" can accept, and what he must reject.

The second approach, which most Nietzsche scholars adopt, views Nietzsche as partly a 'Nazi', arguing that some of the philosopher's tenets are Nazi (such as his rejection of Christianity, his radically aristocratic politics, his Superman and Master Race concepts, his glorification of war), and some are not (such as his anti-nationalism and anti-statism), thus considering that the Nazis were Nietzschean "revisionists", appropriating from the philosopher whatever served their propaganda and disregarding everything which ran counter to the Nazi creed. Scholars such as Crane Brinton and Arthur Knight belong to this category, the latter interpreting Nietzsche's concept of the Superman as Darwinian. But the most prominent Nietzsche scholar in this category remains William Bluhm, who considered that the charges against Nietzsche as the precursor of Nazism were partly true and partly false, because there were two doctrines of Nazism, one for the few, the initiated, the elite, which was very much Nietzschean, and one for the many, the average man, the crowds, which was not; in other words, esoteric versus exoteric Nazism. According to

3

Bluhm, the exoteric doctrine of Nazism focused on German nationalism, biological Aryan racism, and anti-Semitism. As for statism, Bluhm did specify that "state idolatry", which the anti-Nazi Nietzsche scholars use as an argument against any connection between the two philosophies, was not part of Nazi ideology, the latter –unlike Fascism- putting race above state, and considering the state as a mere instrument for the preservation and enhancement of the race. The second Nazi doctrine, the esoteric one, much deeper than the first, espoused the same sort of aristocratic spiritual racism that Nietzsche professed: it was radically elitist yet universal in character, not merely limited to genes.

In the third category of Nietzsche scholars, we find those who view Nietzsche's philosophy as anti-Nazi, a refutation of anything the Nazis believed in, accusing the Nazis of completely distorting what Nietzsche meant to say. Refusing to see any similarity between Nietzsche and Nazism, these scholars view them as two sharply distinct doctrines. Some of these scholars even went as far as to come up with the preposterous and ludicrous affirmation that Nietzsche, the radical aristocrat, was a humanist (according to George Morgan and Walter Kaufmann, the latter having advancing a "spiritual-allegorical" interpretation of Nietzsche), a liberal (according to the existentialist Karl Jaspers), or even a socialist (according to H. Lefebvre, who saw that the ideas of Nietzsche fall into the Marxian conception of man)!! The scholars who fall into this category and hence deny the Nietzschean-Nazi connection, mainly base their allegations on the fact that Nietzsche was strongly anti-political, anti-statist, anti-nationalist, that he considered racial-mixing a natural phenomenon sometimes beneficial to culture, and that he felt no hostility whatsoever towards the Jews, what's more, that he even "admired" them…

Beyond the controversy: Nietzsche and "Esoteric Nazism"

In response to such allegations, I argue that Nietzsche's anti-political, anti-nationalist and anti-statist philosophy was not in the least contradictory with the spiritual, supra-national racism of the Nazis, which was an integral and essential part of the Nazi esoteric doctrine Bluhm was referring to, though this side of Nazism was less apparent than the exoteric, demagogic, nationalist discourse meant for popular consumption and the mobilisation of the masses. Racism and nationalism are indeed two different, often contrasting, ideologies (a nation being a cultural-geographical unit, whereas race is an anthropological-spiritual, i.e. supra-national unit), and the Nazis were essentially racist, yet they tried to combine and reconcile these two theories, coming up with a unique blend, "racist nationalism" (the *Voelkish* State, a primitive, organic, and racial and spiritual community or "Gemeinschaft", as opposed to the modern political and multi-racial Nation-State or "Gesellschaft", based on the Social Contract)... "Racist nationalism" thus aimed at reconciling race with nation (by achieving a racially pure nation), purifying the German race of all non-Germanic elements, such as the Alpine or Mediterranean elements, in order to return to the racial basis of the ancient German Nation which was primarily Aryan, or Nordic; i.e., to make Germany, the original homeland of the Aryans, the new spiritual centre of the Aryans of the world. Indeed, although Nazism was viewed outwardly as a nationalist movement, its real theory of the state was universal in character, based on a racist-aristocratic-mystical view of the world, for the Nazi state was not an end in itself (unlike fascism), what Nietzsche termed "the coldest of cold monsters", rather a means to a higher end, namely the breeding and perpetuation of Nietzsche's Master Race, a universal race of Supermen transcending political and national boundaries.

Furthermore, I argue that even Nietzsche's well-known hatred for the Germans could be explained, after close analysis, as hatred towards the Judaeo-Christian, Liberal, un-Germanic elements in the modern German character, and hostility towards what Nietzsche viewed as the Reich's relatively Liberal tendencies... It is worth noting in this respect that Nietzsche often contrasted the authentic German, the ancient pagan Teuton (*Der Germane* as opposed to *Der Deutsche*), the "magnificent blond Beast", whom he admired, with the modern Liberal, Christian, "domesticated", weakened, and atypical German.

Finally, I argue that Nietzsche was a virulent "spiritual" and pagan anti-Semite, i.e., that he morally despised the Jews as the decadents of humanity and falsifiers of history, as the living incarnation of the slave morality. Nietzsche was indeed thoroughly hostile to the Jewish Semitic spirit which he saw as the perfect antithesis to the Indo-European or Aryan spirit, best represented by the Vedic, Zoroastrian, and the Dionysian religions, and, what's more, he often contrasted the Aryan and Semitic spirits as Master versus Slave moralities, praising the superiority of Aryan humanity and civilisation (Manu, founder of the first Aryan religion, the Aryan Vedas, Zarathustra, Brahmanism's racial hierarchical caste system, the "Blond Beast", ...). What could be more racist and anti-Semitic?

Nevertheless, the fact is that the controversy over the Nietzschean-Nazi relationship still lingers to this day, each "school" of Nietzsche scholars firmly clinging to its interpretation, even though all agree that, misinterpreted or not, Nietzsche's greatest political influence has been on the Nazi ideology, and that the parallel between the two doctrines is a very close one… By showing the shortages in all three interpretations of the Nietzsche-Nazi relationship, this book's contribution lies in its attempt to transcend the said controversy, introducing a new interpretation of the Nietzsche-Nazi connection which consists of a comparison between the philosopher's writings and the Nazi esoteric doctrine which, I argue, was purely Nietzschean, contrary to the exoteric one whose relationship to the Nietzschean doctrine is more controversial.

[handwritten margin note, left: so there were no other influences / contradiction to earlier statement]

[handwritten margin note, right: they've compared the external Nazism not the main doctrine]

… Indeed, the main shortage in the Nietzschean scholars' different interpretations lies in the fact that the latter have compared Nietzsche and the exoteric side of Nazism, not paying heed to the esoteric, real meaning of the Nazi ideology, the "other side" of Nazism… These scholars have misinterpreted and have failed to grasp the deeper, inner meaning and essence of National Socialism, which, according to Hitler, and as I shall demonstrate throughout this work, was much more than a political movement, even "more than a religion: it is the will to create a New Man", a superhuman being who symbolises the culmination of evolution. What could be more Nietzschean? In fact, the creation of this Superman as humanity's highest purpose was -and here lies the significance of this book- also Nietzsche's highest goal, the pillar and cornerstone of his doctrine…

Although Bluhm was the first among the cited scholars to specify that Nazism had an esoteric elitist doctrine far deeper than the nationalist mass-politics, he nonetheless failed to go into an in-depth analysis of Esoteric National Socialism (merely mentioning that this doctrine was supra-nationalist, based on a racism that was spiritual, not biological) and hence he was unable to establish a solid link between Nietzsche and Nazism's "other doctrine". Bluhm was also mistaken in his rather hasty conclusion that, to the Nazis, race was solely psychological, not based on genes. In the chapter which discusses Nazism's theory of race, I will show that the exoteric and esoteric doctrines of Nazism were indeed different, yet they were not contradictory (in contrast to what Bluhm assumes), the latter having a deeper meaning than the former: for example, "racist nationalism" was a synthesis of a superior nation and a superior race; also, the concept of race for Nazism was psychological as well as biological, i.e. mystic-biological, which means that the biological factor was a pre-condition for the psychological or spiritual factor. In other words, as

6

H.S. Chamberlain put it, race was much more a spiritual matter than a biological matter, yet to him biology was an important prerequisite for racial superiority: an Aryan spirit could indeed be incarnated in a non-Aryan body, yet this latter should contain a certain amount of Aryan blood to "receive" a superior soul. In the Nazi esoteric doctrine, spirit had precedence over biology, the latter being a vehicle for the former, yet biology was essential, for the Nazis -like Nietzsche- believed in the unity of body and spirit: hence, a superior Aryan soul could only dwell in an Aryan -or at least half-Aryan- body... contrary to Bluhm's own rather hasty interpretation of Nazism's "esoteric racism"...

Having criticised Bluhm's theory and its shortcomings, my own theory starts where Bluhm's theory ends: first, by unveiling the Nazi "Secret Doctrine" and second, by establishing the link between Esoteric Nazism and Nietzsche's philosophy, in order to demonstrate in a concrete manner that the Nazis were true Nietzscheans and not mere revisionists... In doing so, I will analyse Nazism esoterically, for there is where the real doctrine lies.

Although the Nietzschean-Nazi connection remains a controversial one among scholars, yet when we penetrate deeper into the philosopher's thought as well as Nazism's supranational elitist-spiritual racism, we find clear, even striking philosophical, moral and spiritual affinities. Hence, we can infer that all the concrete and reliable evidence that will be presented throughout this book will support my main assumption, which is the following: it is an undeniable fact that the Nazis were true and pure Nietzscheans, and we cannot but acknowledge the hard reality that the Nazis were directly and profoundly influenced by Nietzsche, whom they rightfully considered their prophet, turning him into the Third Reich's most important philosopher, thus compelling a well-known scholar to affirm: *"the relation of Fascism to Nietzsche recalls the relation of the French Revolution to Rousseau"* (2) ... or the relation of Leninism to Marx...

CHAPTER TWO

THE REVIVAL OF ARYAN PAGANISM

almost Platonic →
'superhumans' / Gods

"We few or many who dare again to live in a dismoralised world, we pagans in faith: we are also the first to grasp what a pagan faith is: -to have to imagine higher creatures than man, but beyond good and evil; to have to consider all being higher as also being immoral. We believe in Olympus- and not in the 'Crucified'."

Roman/Greek Gods

Jesus

Friedrich Nietzsche

"Do you understand now the profound significance of our National Socialist movement? Whoever sees in National Socialism nothing but a political movement does not know much about it... It is even higher than a religion: it is the will to create mankind anew."

Adolf Hitler

dismissing the importance of religion

the Nazi regime is more important

they are the beings 'higher' than men

A. Nietzsche, Nazism and neo-paganism

The modern revival of paganism in Germany by the German romantic movement as well as German nationalism, after the reunification of the Nation in the 19th century, served to prove the superiority of the Aryan Master Race. Indeed, German neo-paganism calls for a return to the pre-Christian, Aryan "Natural Religion" of the ancient pagan Germans, a pantheistic religion mainly based on the belief in an "inner God" immanent in nature and man's soul, on Germanic mythology and its veneration of god-men or Supermen; a religion which embodied the aristocratic principle of nature, i.e. the fundamental inequality between species (human beings included), which gives the stronger the natural right to dominate the weaker in a process of natural selection for the perpetual breeding of higher species... The pagan man, the man of Antiquity, a strong and proud warrior alien to the anti-natural and egalitarian values of Judaism and Christianity, was also a model for both Nietzsche and the Nazis, who were staunch neo-pagans, for he incarnated the Superman in every aspect, i.e. the healthy aristocrat, the Higher Man, superior in body and spirit... The Indo-European noble or Brahmin, the Greek, the Spartan, the ancient German, the Roman (of whom Nietzsche wrote in his Genealogy of Morals: *"nobody stronger and nobler has yet existed on earth or even been dreamed of"*) (1)... were all viewed by Nietzsche as well as the Nazis as superior men of a distinct species, a tough breed of masters who "lived according to nature" -and its aristocratic principle of the survival of the strongest- as much as possible.

It is worth noting that neo-paganism, although thoroughly opposed to Judaeo-Christianity, is nonetheless essentially a spiritual movement which advocates a revival of the ancient spiritual tradition rooted in the most remote depths of humanity's collective memory. This explains Nietzsche's (and later Nazism's) unique "spiritual" brand of atheism, what Schopenhauer termed "noble atheism", a fact which didn't go unnoticed by Bruce Detwiler, a Nietzsche scholar, who remarked: *"it is indeed paradoxical that Western spirituality in the twentieth century has been so influenced- indeed, awakened- by a man who declared the death of God and who defined himself as the Antichrist... Nietzsche becomes Western philosophy's first avowed atheist of the far Right"* (2). It is in the same spirit that Heinrich Himmler, head of the S.S. (*Schutzstaffeln*), Nazi Germany's pagan aristocracy, declared that his SS were *Gottgläubig* ("believers in God"), though to him, the nature of this All-powerful Force and Man's relation to it was radically different from the Judaeo-Christian transcendent and anthropomorphic conception of God... For the Nazi top elite, which was obsessed with mysticism, Man had an intimate relationship with God, and therefore the union with the divinity was an attainable goal for a few higher men.

Hence, both Nietzsche and the Nazis called for a revival of paganism, the "cult of Antiquity", "*for in the world of antiquity,*", says Nietzsche, "*there reigned a different, more lordly morality than today; and the man of antiquity, raised in this morality, was a stronger and deeper man than the man of today-he alone has hitherto been 'the man that has turned out well'* " (3). Nietzsche, who praised the pagan "*old, noble taste, the agonal instinct, the polis, the value of the race, the authority of tradition*" (4), saw himself as the incarnation of Zarathustra, the Persian prophet, and was firmly convinced that the neo-pagan spiritual message for mankind that he was carrying would make greatness possible again in this modern mediocre world, by imposing a revaluation of modernity's "human, all-too human" Judaeo-Christian values:

> "*We few or many who again dare to live in a dismoralised world, we pagans in faith: we are probably also the first to grasp what a pagan faith is:- to have to imagine higher creatures than man, but beyond good and evil; to have to consider all being higher as also being immoral. We believe in Olympus- and not in the "Crucified*" (5).

Likewise, the Nazis were firmly convinced that they were the representatives of a new political faith (Nazism), a new paganism which would replace outdated Judaeo-Christian beliefs and ceremonies: "*the enthusiasm of the people for the parades and torchlight processions and the almost unbearable emotionalism of the* (pagan) *ceremonies were all alike impressive*" (6). The Nazi religion, a modern mythology of occultism, was indeed a real "spiritual revolution" in European culture, a new vision of the universe heralding the advent of a New Age for mankind. Hitler, the "Occult Messiah", was in fact proclaiming a wonderful millennial future for the Aryan race when he announced:

> "*We are at the outset of a tremendous revolution in moral ideas and man's spiritual orientation. A new age of the magic interpretation of the world is coming, an interpretation in terms of will and not the intellect*" (7).

will to power?
struggle?

B. Esoteric Nazism: breeding the God-Man, or Nietzsche's Superman

It is worth noting here that by showing the link between Nietzsche's philosophy and Nazi ideology, I am at the same time unveiling the Nazi "Secret Doctrine", i.e. "Esoteric Nazism" not found in Hitler's "Mein Kampf" or his public speeches, addressed to the uninitiated masses, but rather in the Fuehrer's secret conversations with the Nazi top elite and based on occult sources related to the whole Aryanist spiritual school of thought, from the Vedas to Theosophy. Indeed, it would be an elementary mistake to dismiss or underrate the importance of the influence of Aryan occultism (the code of Manu, the Vedic philosophy, Brahmanism, Zoroastrianism, the cults of Greek deities, ...) on both the Nietzschean doctrine and Nazi ideology, the latter being a truly unique phenomenon combining, for the first time in history, spiritualism and politics, or, as Hitler liked to say, esoteric knowledge with esoteric power. As Hermann Rauschning affirmed, *"it is impossible to understand Hitler's political plans unless one is familiar with his basic beliefs and his conviction that there is a magic relationship between Man and the Universe"* (8).

Hitler, who considered that *"the aim of human evolution is to attain a mystic vision of the Universe"* (9), also repeatedly assured Rauschning that true Nazism was much deeper than was widely believed:

"Do you understand now the profound significance of our National-Socialist movement? Whoever sees in National Socialism nothing but a political movement doesn't know much about it ... It is even more than a religion: it is the will to create mankind anew" (10).

Indeed, Nazism was deeply imbued with occultism, and the hypothesis of a community of Initiates beneath the cloak of National Socialism is gradually gaining ground in academic circles, following the publication of a good number of books linking Nazism with Aryan mysticism and occultism, the same sources which inspired Nietzsche's pagan philosophy.

Mystic writers like professor Karl Haushofer (who, according to Rudolph Hess, was the *"secret 'Master Magician of the Nazi party', the man behind Hitler"*), Lanz von Liebenfels, Karl-Maria Wiligut, Rudolf von Sebottendorf, Meister Eckhart, Dietrich Eckart, George Gurdjieff, Aleister Crowley, Carl Gustav Jung, H.S. Chamberlain, Richard

Wagner, Guido von List, Herbert Reichstein, the German scientist Hans Hoerbiger... were the direct or indirect spiritual mentors of the Nazi movement. Lanz von Liebenfels, a mystic racist who founded the Order of the New Templars and preached "theozoology" (a blend of Aryan racism and mysticism), said of the Fuehrer:

> *"Hitler is one of our pupils... you will one day experience that he, and through him we, will one day be victorious, and develop a movement that will make the world tremble..." (11).*

Secret societies like the Order of the New Templars, the Hermetic order of the Golden Dawn, the modern Rosy-Cross, the Luminous Lodge of the Vril Society, the Thule Gesellschaft, the Edda Society, and the Germanenorden, had a tremendous influence on Nazi ideology, and were

> *"more or less closely associated with the powerful and well-organised Theosophical Society (founded by Helena P. Blavatsky, and based on Aryan paganism). Theosophy added to neo-pagan magic an oriental setting and a Hindu terminology... Theosophy was the name finally given to the whole vast renaissance in the world of magic that affected many thinkers so profoundly at the beginning of the century" (12).*

Thus, National-Socialism was linked to occultism:

> *"The remarkable story of the rise of Nazism is implicitly linked to the power of the supernatural... Nazism cannot have been the mere product of socio-economic factors... the myth of a Nazi link with the Orient was of theosophical provenance" (13).*

The S.S., Nazi Germany's political and racial aristocracy, incarnated Nazism's true nature and purpose, i.e., that of a religious pagan order dedicated to fulfilling the ultimate aim of the Aryan millenarian mission, namely the breeding of a new superhuman species, the God-man or culmination of evolution; in other words, Nietzsche's Superman. Indeed, it was Himmler who was entrusted with the task of organising the S.S.:

> *"not as a police force, but as a religious order with a regular hierarchy... Among the highest ranking officials were those in charge of a Black Order... Within the party reference was made to those who were members of 'the inner circle'... It seems certain that the doctrine, never fully defined, was based on an absolute belief in powers that surpassed ordinary human powers. In religion theology, which is considered a science, is distinguished from mysticism which is intuitive and incommunicable. The Ahnenerbe*

14

Society represented the theological, and the Black Order the mystical aspect of the religion of the Lords of Thule." (14).

Himmler, who transformed the S.S. from Hitler's personal bodyguard in the 1920s into an elite unit of crack troops ruthlessly dedicated to the Nazi ideology, was in fact fulfilling Hitler's dream of a new Order of Teutonic Knights, a new Templar Order of Aryan Supermen, a dream the Fuehrer expressed in 1934 when he declared to his confident, Hermann Rauschning: *"we shall form an Order, the Brotherhood of the Templars around the Holy Grail of the pure blood"* (15), a spiritual and racial hierarchical order representing an exact replica of Nietzsche's highest ideal on earth, namely the highly elitist racial caste systems of Manu and Brahmanism (on top of which ruled the Aryan "Masters" over non-Aryan races).

The S.S. was hence a totally independent entity, a "state within a state", based upon esoteric principles:

"The Death's Head SS training in the Burgs learned that 'the only living being that exists is the cosmos or universe. Everything else and all other beings, including Man, are only the various forms… of the living universe'. SS men were instructed in their glorious mission, to create a New Age, a New Order, a New Man, in cooperation with the evolution of the cosmos, and they swore vows which proclaimed their allegiance to an 'irreversible superhuman destiny'…" (16)

We are reminded of Nietzsche's concept of self-overcoming as the universe's sole purpose and mankind's highest and ultimate goal; indeed, according to Nietzsche, man is only a bridge to the Superman, and thus his *raison d'être* lies in his eternal quest to overcome his humanity by creating "something beyond himself": the Superman, the only true meaning of the earth.

An astonishing phenomenon was indeed taking place in the very rationalist and materialist 20th century, and in one of the most industrialised nations of the developed world, Germany, where a political and spiritual movement was venerating and practising an ancient Aryan pagan faith:

"For the broad mass of SS men, there was a compulsory pagan religion based upon these rites which was derived from the occultism of List and Liebenfels. The SS celebrated the festivals of the Nordic pagans… pagan rites replaced the Christian ceremonies" (17).

Furthermore, the emblem of the SS, the double-S sign, the Sig-rune representing "Sowelu" (the sun), was taken from the ancient Nordic runic alphabet. A symbol of light and order against the forces of chaos and darkness, the Sig-rune embodied the male energy,

"life-force, vitality, the light of truth, human consciousness, rationality… the chariot of the gods was often depicted among the Germanic peoples as carrying a sun-disc or mandala, a universal symbol for the sun, the higher self, wholeness" (18).

The Sig-rune symbolised man's need for a deeper spirituality, his need to contact his inner life (we shall later see the similarity of this sign with another Aryan pagan symbol, the Swastika). The meaning of this rune bears a striking resemblance with Nietzsche's three main concepts of the Solar Cult, the Aryan male religion (as opposed to the Lunar Cult, or what Nietzsche termed the "Semitic female religion" of Christianity); the Higher Self (or Nietzsche's "Higher Man"); and Wholeness (represented by Dionysus, the "whole man" in contrast to "fragmentary men"). It is worth noting, in this respect, that Nietzsche always praises the Sun in his writings (especially in his masterpiece, *Zarathustra*), showing his veneration for this symbol of light and truth, and that he often referred to the "Lightning" (the S-rune) as the symbol of the Superman.

C. Aryan paganism: the esoteric tradition from India to Greece

The pre-Christian paganism which Nietzsche and Nazism were preaching was essentially Aryanist, i.e. it was based on Aryan spirituality, on the Aryan esoteric tradition or Theosophy (the Secret Doctrine) professed in India, Persia, Egypt and Greece, by Masters like Rama, Krishna, Manu, Zarathustra, Orpheus, Plato, … and later adopted by the mediaeval Knights Templars, the Rosicrucians, and the Teutonic Knights. This same Indo-European tradition thus showed a congruence between Germanic, Hindu, Persian, and Greek doctrines (all Aryan), from the Indo-European Vedas to the Persian Zend Avesta and the Scandinavian Edda.

This Aryan paganism was clear in Nietzsche's writings, which praised Aryan religions and their prophets and gods such as Manu, the first Aryan lawgiver whose law-book Nietzsche considered an "incomparably spiritual and superior work" representing Aryan humanity "at its best" (19); the

, Nietsche uns he superman?

Persian prophet Zarathustra, whom Nietzsche identified himself with, and whom Rosenberg, the Nazi philosopher, saw as the founder of a "truly Aryan religion"; Dionysus, Prometheus, … deities also worshipped by the National Socialists, who proudly declared themselves Aryanists.

Nietzsche bluntly proved himself an Aryanist when he proclaimed:

"Dare now to be tragic men, for ye are to be redeemed! Ye are to accompany the Dionysian festive procession from India to Greece!" (20),

in a clear reference to the pre-Christian pagan Aryanist tradition to which both he and the Nazis belonged to, as shown in the following themes:

The Hyperboreans or Atlanteans: the original Aryan race

When Nietzsche said: *"Let us look one another in the face. We are Hyperboreans…'Neither by land nor by sea shalt thou find the road to the Hyperboreans': Pindar already knew that of us. Beyond the North, beyond the ice, beyond death"* (21), he was alluding to a deeply spiritual subject, more specifically to Greek mythology, which spoke of the Hyperboreans as *"the race dwelling beyond the north wind"*, in Boreas, a country of warmth and plenty said to be the original homeland of mankind, more specifically of the Aryan race, and probably located in Northern Europe, according to the legend. Apollo was in fact the Hyperborean god of the sun, according to the Greeks.

Likewise, Nazi ideology taught that the Hyperboreans (and the Atlanteans) were the original Aryan race, and were highly civilised and gifted creatures. In the same light, the Thule Gesellschaft (Thule Society), who *"was revealed to be the secret directing agent of the Third Reich"* (22), was named after the supposed original homeland of the Hyperboreans, an island (Thule) which was thought to have *"disappeared somewhere in the extreme North"*:

"Off Greeland? Off Labrador? Like Atlantis, Thule was thought to have been the magic centre of a vanished civilisation. Eckart and his friends believed that not all the secrets of Thule had perished. Beings intermediate between Man and other intelligent Beings from Beyond, would place at the disposal of the Initiates a reservoir of forces which could be drawn upon to enable Germany to dominate the world again and be the cradle of the coming race of Supermen which would result from mutations of the human species." (23).

Occultists thus believed that Thule had once been the source of the occult wisdom of the "Northern Mystery Tradition".

The Greek world: the pagan ideal

"The Greeks, the hitherto highest type of man"

[handwritten: weak comparison]

Friedrich Nietzsche

"I am Greek..."

[handwritten: three words?]

Adolf Hitler

For both Nietzsche and the Nazis, it was the Greek world, the "perfect world", which represented paganism at its best, as this passage from Nietzsche's last major work, "The Will to Power", shows :

> *"One is no longer at home anywhere; at last one belongs back to that place in which alone one can be at home, because it is the only place which one would want to be at home: the Greek world!... A few centuries hence, perhaps, one will judge that all German philosophy derives its real dignity from being a gradual reclamation of the soil of antiquity, and that all claims to "originality" must sound petty and ludicrous in relation to that higher claim of the Germans to have joined anew the bond that seemed to be broken, the bond with the Greeks, the hitherto highest type of man" (24).*

Nietzsche in fact considered that perfection lay in the unity between the deities of Apollo and Dionysus, the former symbolising order and reason, the latter eternal creation and spirituality.

It was the Nazis who tried to "join anew" this "bond with the Greeks", with the Greek spirit and philosophy, i.e. the "real Aryan spirit" deriving from the Indo-European, Greco-Roman tradition, as opposed to the Judaeo-Christian spirit of Western civilisation. Nazi Germany was indeed a self-proclaimed "New Greece": the colossal Greek-style architectural plans Hitler had designed for Berlin testify to this Nazi fascination with Greece, compelling Carl Gustav Jung, the great mystic psychologist, to speak of the "*tyranny of Greece over Germany*" (25), a "spiritual tyranny" imposed by the Nazi regime. When asked by Leon Degrelle, the commander of the SS Belgian brigade "Wallonie", whether he felt he was a German or a European, Hitler gave this most astonishing answer: *"I am Greek"*... meaning to say that he was the inheritor of the Greek spirit, which itself had inherited the Aryan Indian and Persian spiritual message found in the Vedas and the Zend Avesta.

The legend of Prometheus: the Aryan spirit at its best

"The tale of Prometheus is an original possession of the entire Aryan family of races and documentary evidence of their capacity for the profoundly tragic"

Friedrich Nietzsche

"The Aryan is the Prometheus of mankind"

Adolf Hitler

Thus, for both Nietzsche and the Nazis, the Greek world embodied the pagan ideal, for it was in accordance with the aristocratic principle of nature. Greek gods were the living embodiment of this sublime spirit of a higher Aryan humanity. The "manly" Aryan legend of Prometheus of Aeschylus, which Nietzsche praised in this passage from his "Birth of Tragedy", contrasting it with the "feminine" Semitic legend of the Fall of Man, well illustrates this spirit and best exemplifies Aryan Man's quest for union with God:

"Man, elevating himself to the rank of the Titans, acquires his culture by his own efforts and compels the gods to unite with him, because in his self-sufficient wisdom he has their existence and their limits in his hand... The tale of Prometheus is an original possession of the entire Aryan family of races and documentary evidence for their capacity for the profoundly tragic. Indeed, it is not improbable that this myth has the same characteristic significance for the Aryan race that the myth of the fall of man has for the Semitic... The best and highest that men can acquire they obtain by a crime, and must now in their turn take upon themselves its consequences, namely the whole flood of sufferings and sorrows with which the offended celestials must visit the nobly aspiring race of man: a bitter reflection, which, by the dignity it confers on crime, contrasts strangely with the Semitic myth of the fall of man, in which curiosity, beguilement, seducibility, wantonness- in short, a whole series of pre-eminently feminine passions- were regarded as the origin of evil. What distinguishes the Aryan representation is the sublime view of active sin as the properly Promethean virtue... With the heroic effort made by the individual for universality, in his attempt to pass beyond individuation and become the one universal being, he experiences in himself the primordial contradiction concealed in the essence of things, i.e.,

Genesis 1 & 2 -> Adam & Eve

he trespasses and suffers. Accordingly crime is understood by the Aryans to be a man, sin by the Semites a woman; as also, the original crime is committed by man, the original sin by woman... the innermost core of the tale of Prometheus [is] the necessity of crime imposed on the titanically striving individual" (26).

The male active sin, represented by the Aryan Prometheus, is contrasted with the female passive sin conceived by Semitic Judaeo-Christianity. Nietzsche's Aryanism, which is very much obvious in this passage, has curiously, carefully, and conveniently been overlooked by scholars -like Walter Kaufmann- who deny the Nietzsche-Nazi connection... As for the Nazi adoption of the Promethean myth, it is clearly shown by Hitler's following famous passage in Mein Kampf, in which he describes the Aryan as the Prometheus of humanity:

"The Aryan is the Prometheus of mankind from whose bright forehead the divine spark of genius has sprung at all times, forever kindling anew that fire of knowledge which illuminated the night of silent mysteries and thus caused man to climb the path to mastery over the other beings of this earth. Exclude him- and perhaps after a few thousand years darkness will again descend on the earth, human culture will pass, and the world turn to a desert" (27).

According to Theosophy (which greatly inspired the Nazi ideology), the term Prometheus derives from Prometheia: *"fore-knowledge, forethought"*. Helena Petrovna Blavatsky, founder of the Theosophical Society, suggests a deeper Aryanist meaning to the word, linking it with the Swastika:

"We may find, in searching, a more poetical origin for the 'fire bringer' than that displayed in its Sanskrit origin. The Svastica, sacred sign and instrument for kindling sacred fire, may explain it better. Prometheus, the fire-bringer, is the Pramantha personified... He finds his prototype in the Aryan Matarisvan, a divine... personage, closely associated with the fire god of the Veda, Agni" (28).

In the aforementioned passage, the Promethean legend, venerated by Nietzsche, is linked to the Swastika, the first Aryan religious sign which the Nazis adopted as their emblem. Therefore, before endeavouring to trace the similarities between the Promethean legend and the significance of the Swastika, we must first unveil the true meaning of this Nazi symbol.

Prometheus and the Swastika: Aryan symbols for the God-Man

The Swastika, or Svastika, (a Sanskrit word for "Sun", "life"), the instrument for kindling sacred fire, the symbol of the Sun, of light, of supreme truth, of wholeness -in short, of perfection- was a holy Aryan sign, *"since it derived from the Feuerquirl (fire whisk) with which Mundelfori had initially twirled the cosmos into being"* (29). In Nazi Germany, the worship of nature, particularly of the life-giving power of the sun, *"was symbolised in the ubiquitous display of the Swastika, the archetype of Nazi emblems. The Nordic inheritance of the German people was to be reinstated after centuries of Christian distortion and error"* (30). Hitler, who saw in the Swastika *"the mission of the struggle for the victory of the Aryan man, and, by the same token, the victory of the idea of creative work"* (31), was by the same token expressing his veneration for a sign related to both the wheel and the cross, what Jung describes as *"a pagan sun symbol... found all over the earth: it is an exceedingly archaic sun symbol"* (32).

The Swastika *"has always been considered a magic sign... It is an exclusively Aryan symbol"* (33). Owing to the Aryan invasions of large parts of Southern Asia, Tibet is *"one of the countries in the world where the Swastika... is most commonly met with"* (34). This explains the amazing discovery the Russians made when they took Berlin in 1945, where *"they found to their astonishment one thousand Tibetan corpses in German army uniforms"* (35); thousands of miles away from their homeland, these Tibetans (in addition to thousands of non-German members of the SS from over 17 other nations) chose to die for the sake of the Aryan millenarian spiritual cause which the Nazis undertook to fulfil on behalf of all Aryan humanity ... Given these facts, how can Walter Kaufmann still affirm that Nazism was a purely nationalistic movement, thus denying its universal scope?

Going back to our identification of the promethean myth with the Swastika, we find that this sign's profound meaning also encompasses the purely Aryan concepts of the God-Man, the sacred fire of truth, and the Aryan solar cult typified by the Promethean myth... The following passage by Blavatsky helps explain this congruence:

"Applied to the Microcosm, Man, it (the Swastika) shows him to be a link between heaven and Earth: the right hand being raised at the end of a horizontal arm, the left pointing to the Earth.... It is not too much to say that the compound symbolism of this universal and most suggestive of signs contains the key to the seven great mysteries of Kosmos. Born in the mystical conception of the early Aryans, and by them placed

at the very threshold of eternity, on the head of the serpent Ananta, it found its spiritual death in the scholastic interpretations of mediaeval Anthropomorphists. It is the Alpha and the Omega of universal creative Force, evolving from pure Spirit and ending in gross Matter. It is also the key to the cycle of Science, divine and human; and he who comprehends its full meaning is for ever liberated from the toils of Mahamaya, the great Illusion and Deceiver" (36).

In short, the Swastika is the symbol of man's divine nature, of truth (symbolised by the sun, the fire or the light), of life, and therefore reminds us of the Promethean legend as described earlier by Nietzsche, in which Prometheus, the man who defied the gods by stealing the sacred fire (truth, divine knowledge) from them, thus became a universal man, a God-Man. Both the Swastika and Nietzsche's Prometheus show the fundamental unity of the microcosm (Man) and the macrocosm (the Universe), a unity embodied by the Superman.

Nietzsche's "Eternal Recurrence" and the Nazi racial theory of evolutionary cycles

Another important feature of the Aryan paganism Nietzsche and the Nazis professed was what Nietzsche termed the "Eternal Recurrence", which is closely linked to the Hindu-inspired theosophical theory of evolutionary cycles or "root-races" adopted by the Nazis. For Nietzsche,

"everything goes, everything returns; the wheel of existence rolls for ever. Everything dies, everything blossoms anew… The middle is everywhere. The path of eternity is crooked" (37).

"Energy", says Nietzsche, "was once thought to be unlimited. Now we know that it is limited. It is eternally active, but it cannot eternally create new forms. Therefore it must repeat itself… (38).

For Nietzsche, however, the Eternal Recurrence is not simply an aimless circular conception of time: we shall see in the next chapter how Nietzsche's thought of return is that of creative progress ultimately leading to the Superman… But, for now, let us simply note that this Nietzschean cyclical conception of history is similar to the theosophical doctrine of evolutionary cosmic cycles and root-races to which the Nazis adhered. The Nazis in fact believed -as Nietzsche did- in the rule of periodicity, whereby all creation is subject to an endless cycle of destruction and rebirth. These rounds always terminate at a level spiritually superior to their starting-point. For the Nazi elite, indeed, Man was organically linked to the cosmos, and

"not only was humanity assigned an age of far greater antiquity than that conceded by science, but it was also integrated into a scheme of cosmic, physical, and spiritual evolution... Each round witnessed the rise and fall of seven consecutive root-races, which descended on the scale of spiritual development from the first to the fourth, becoming increasingly enmeshed in the material world (the Gnostic notion of a Fall from Light into Darkness was quite explicit), before ascending through progressively superior root-races from the fifth to the seventh... Present humanity constituted the fifth root-race upon a planet that was passing through the fourth cosmic round, so that a process of spiritual advance lay before the species. The fifth root-race was called the Aryan race and had been preceded by the fourth root-race of the Atlanteans, which had largely perished in a flood that submerged their mid-Atlantic continent" (39).

This theosophical racial theory of human evolution, which the Nazis adopted, is reminiscent of Nietzsche's concept of Eternal Recurrence. *—evidence?*

Furthermore, the Nazis also believed in reincarnation and karma, concepts that are closely linked to Nietzsche's doctrine of Eternal Recurrence... Finally, the Swastika, in addition to symbolising the sun, is also called the "hammer of creation" and thus represents "eternal or perpetual creation", i.e. a cyclical view of time:

"In the macrocosmic work, the "Hammer of Creation", with its four arms bent at right angles, refers to the continual motion and revolution of the invisible Kosmos of Forces. In that of the manifested Kosmos and our Earth, it points to the rotation in the cycles of Time of the world's axes and their equatorial belts; the two lines forming the svastica meaning Spirit and Matter, the four hooks suggesting the motion in the revolving cycles" (40).

D. Neo-paganism: the Aryan Christ versus Semitic Judaeo-Christianity

Christ, the hero, versus Christianity, the "anti-Aryan religion"

"Christianity is the ultimate Jewish consequence... the anti-Aryan, anti-pagan religion par excellence".

"Is the pagan cult not a form of thanksgiving and affirmation of life? Must its highest representative not be an apology for and deification of life? The type of a well constituted and ecstatically overflowing spirit! ... Dionysus versus the Crucified: there you have the antithesis"

[handwritten: greek God] [handwritten: Christ] [handwritten: Not damning Jews]

Friedrich Nietzsche

"Judaeo-Christianity, the greatest plague delivered by history"

Heinrich Himmler

"National Socialism and Christianity are irreconcilable"

Martin Bormann

"One is either a German or a Christian. You cannot be both"

Alfred Rosenberg

The Aryan neo-paganism that Nietzsche and the Nazis professed led both of them to reject Judaeo-Christianity as a Semitic religion, the "ultimate Jewish consequence" and the "anti-Aryan religion *par excellence*" in Nietzsche's exact words. Therefore, it was only natural for Nietzsche (and later the Nazis) to contrast the pagan and the Christian spirits, best exemplified respectively by Dionysus and the "Crucified":

"The two types: Dionysus and the Crucified... but are we not omitting one type of religious man, the pagan? Is the pagan cult not a form of thanksgiving and affirmation of life? Must its highest representative not be an apology for and deification of life? The type of a well-constituted and ecstatically overflowing spirit! The type of a spirit that takes into itself and redeems the contradictions and questionable aspects of existence! It is here I set the Dionysus of the Greeks: the religious affirmation of life, life whole and not denied or in part... Dionysus versus the "Crucified": there you have the antithesis... It is not a difference in regard to their martyrdom- it is in the meaning of it. Life itself, its eternal fruitfulness and recurrence, creates torment, destruction, the will to annihilation. In the other case, suffering- the "Crucified as the innocent one"- counts as an objection to this life, as a formula for its condemnation... The god on the cross is a curse on life, a signpost to seek redemption from life; Dionysus cut to pieces is a promise of life: it will be eternally reborn and return again from destruction" (41).

When Nietzsche contrasts Dionysus with the "Crucified", he is rejecting the image of the "innocent victim" which the Church has presented to the masses in order to subjugate them, i.e. Christ's humiliating death instead of his heroic life which should serve as a model for the rest of humanity to follow. Therefore, it is worth noting here that although Nietzsche rejected Christianity as the *"ultimate Jewish consequence"*, he did contrast it with the life and practice of the Christ, whom he admired, considering that it was his disciples, mainly Paul, "the Jew, the eternal Jew", and Peter, who distorted Jesus' original teachings, i.e. primitive Christianity, turning them into a religion 'for the sick and the meek'.

Similarly for the Nazis, who, as true pagans, rejected Judaeo-Christianity as a Semitic religion alien to the Aryan heroic spirit, but nonetheless contrasted this religion with the personality and life of Jesus, whom Chamberlain and Rosenberg, Nazi Germany's two most influential philosophers, considered as Aryan by race and spirit, as Rosenberg's following passage testifies:

"The Roman Church has emphasised his submissive humility because it wishes to have as many submissive followers as possible. To correct this is a problem for a German revival. To us, Jesus appears as a lord who is conscious of his lordship in the highest and best sense of the term. It is his life which is significant for Germanic men, not his agonising death, to which he owes his success among Alpine and Mediterranean peoples. We discern in the Gospels the mighty preacher, the man of wrath in the Temple, the man whom all men followed, not the sacrificial lamb of Jewish prophecy, not the crucified one" (42).

[margin note: Jesus' life is good but his 'solution' is false]

Like Nietzsche, therefore, the Nazis contrasted the heroic Christ with the image of the Crucified, which Christianity was based upon. As staunch advocates of neo-paganism, Friedrich Nietzsche and the Nazi elite thus vehemently opposed Judaised Christianity, considering it a transvaluation of pagan, Aryan values:

"Christianity robbed us of the harvest of the culture of the ancient world" (43),

[margin note: over-exaggeration — how does he know?]

writes Nietzsche, exclaiming with indignation:

"The entire work of the ancient world in vain!" (44).

For Nietzsche, indeed, "'Christianity' has become something fundamentally different from what its founder did and desired. It is the great anti-pagan movement of antiquity,... it is the rise of the pessimism of the weak, the inferior, the suffering, the oppressed. Its mortal enemy is (1) power in character, spirit and taste; ... its mortal enemy is the Roman just as much as the Greek" (45),

i..e. the classical ideal and the noble religion. Christianity was therefore the religion of the lower masses, the slaves, the non-noble classes.

Christianity's worst crime, according to Nietzsche, is its corruption of *"the most manly and capable of the human race, the peoples of Northern Europe"*, the pagan Germanic peoples, turning the "magnificent blond beasts of prey", the Vikings, the strong and ruthless warriors, into sick, weak and "good" Christians (46). The exact same condemnation of Christianity was made by the Nazis who considered that the Germans

"had been too long held in bondage by the alien beliefs of a Jewish-derived faith. In the eyes of the Nazis a trilogy had been set up- Rome, Judea and Moscow, and after the other two, Rome was considered the severest enemy of the Nordic Germanic Weltanschauung" (47).

We shall see in Chapter Five how Nietzsche contrasted Rome with Judea as incarnating respectively the Master Morality and the Slave Morality.

In Nietzsche's analysis, decadent Judaeo-Christianity, a grotesque distortion of Christ's own vision, has

"waged a war to the death against this higher type of man, ... it has taken the side of everything weak, base, ill-constituted, it has made an ideal out of opposition to the preservative instincts of strong life" (48)

For Nietzsche, *"the church is precisely that against which Jesus preached- and against which he taught his disciples to fight"* (49)... And thus, Christianity - which ironically took its name from its radically different original founder- and the Church, are regarded by Nietzsche as the exact antitheses to the Gospel, to Christ's spirit and practice, and therefore, the "world-historical irony" lay in the fact *"that mankind should fall on its knees before the opposite of what was the origin, the meaning, the right of the Gospel."* (50).

For the Nazis, too, Judaeo-Christianity was, in Himmler's words, *"the greatest plague delivered by history"* (51), the fact which prompted Martin Bormann, Hitler's secretary, to proudly proclaim that *"National Socialism and Christianity are irreconcilable"* (52) ... Therefore, the Nazis decided that the Christian cross must be removed from all churches, cathedrals and chapels and it must be superseded by the *"only unconquerable symbol, the*

Swastika" (53). Basing their rejection of this Jewish religion on Nietzsche's famous passage in the Antichrist: *"The Cross [Kreuz] as sign... against health, beauty, sense, bravery, intellect, kindliness of soul- against life itself"*, the Nazis suggested it be replaced by *"the Swastika [Hakenkreuz] as sign for health, beauty, sense, bravery, intellect, kindliness of soul- for Life itself"* (54).

[handwritten margin note: must / read Nietesche too similar / assumption]

According to the Nazi elite, Christianity in its present form could not provide the necessary spiritual force needed in the Third Reich, for its crude and static dogmas are alien to the pagan beliefs of the ancient Germanic race.

The National Socialist movement -which the German psychologist Carl Gustav Jung saw as a modern revival of paganism, where *"Wotan* (the supreme deity of the Vikings or Teutons) *the wanderer was on the move"* (Jung not failing to note Wotan's ancient connections with the figures of Christ and Dionysus [55])- advocated a *"Germanic Christianity"*, a return to the Aryan pagan sources of primitive Christianity, to Christ's original message of the "God within", or the God-Man, a message representing the culmination of the pagan spirit, and which was therefore *"alien to the Jewish spirit"*; and, consequently, the Nazi regime sought to bring about the total separation of Christianity from Judaism through the complete elimination from Christianity of all Jewish elements:

"Away with the Old Testament! A Christianity which still clings to the Old Testament is a Jewish religion, irreconcilable with the spirit of the German people" (56).

Jesus Christ, the Aryan rebel against the Jewish spirit

Thus, Nietzsche (and later the Nazis) despised Judaeo-Christianity as *"the anti-Aryan religion par excellence"*, as a Semitic religion which represents *"the revaluation of all Aryan values"* (57), and which is hence unworthy of its founder, Jesus Christ, *"the noblest man"* (58), a *"free spirit"* (59) whose *"un-Jewish, mystical doctrine of the 'Kingdom of Heaven within us'"* the Nazis praised as typically Aryan, while Chamberlain saw in the birth of Jesus Christ the most important date in the whole history of mankind (60):

"The coming of Christ signifies, from the point of view of world's history, the coming of a new human species" (61).

Indeed, for Chamberlain, Jesus, though of Jewish culture and religion, was definitely not a Jew neither by race nor by spirit, implying that pure Aryan blood had been infused into the Galileans who were viewed by the Jews as an alien people:

He was a Jew...

"Christ was no Jew... whoever asserts he is is either ignorant or insincere... There is not the slightest foundation for the supposition that Christ's parents were of Jewish descent... The probability that Christ was no Jew, that he had not a drop of genuinely Jewish blood in his veins, is so great that it is almost equivalent to a certainty" (62).

Chamberlain advanced as concrete proof of Christ's non-Jewish biological and spiritual belonging the fact that, first, Jesus rebelled against Judaism, representing its complete negation (i.e. his spirit was antithetical to the Jewish spirit), and second, that Jesus belonged to the Essenes, a community of Aryan origin.

For Rosenberg, Nazism's philosopher who called for a "Germanic Christianity", contrasting Jesus the Aryan with Paul the Jew, the real Christ was the heroic rebel against the Jewish spirit, a "Son of God" or God-Man, *"in contrast to the Jewish doctrine of the servant of God"* (63), an Aryan Superman who, according to Chamberlain, had brought

"not peace but the sword. The life of Jesus Christ is an open declaration of war, not against the forms of civilisation, culture and religion, which He found around Him- but certainly against the inner spirit of mankind, against the motives which underlie their actions, against the goal which they set for themselves in the future life and in the present" (64). theological evidence doesn't survive

In other words, Christ's message was a call for a spiritual awakening of mankind, for its spiritual rebirth in order to reach perfection and divinity.

Chamberlain goes further in his attempt to prove Christ's heroic" and strong Aryan spirit and identity, thus condemning the "mistaken view" of Jesus held today, by asserting that:

"In the advent of Christ we find the grandest example of heroism. Moral heroism is in Him so sublime that the much-extolled physical courage of heroes seems as nothing; certain it is that only heroic souls- only 'masters'- can in the true sense of the word be Christians. And when Christ says 'I am meek', we well understand that this is the meekness of the hero sure of victory; and when He says, 'I am lowly of heart', we know that this is not the humility of the slave, but the humility of the master, who from the fullness of his power bows down to the weak. On one occasion when Jesus was addressed not simply as Lord or Master, but as 'good master', he rejected the appellation: 'Why callest thou Me good: there is none good' " (65).

Hence, the heroic and mystical spirit of Jesus Christ is sharply contrasted with the Jewish cowardly, materialistic, and base spirit. Hitler in fact says that the

"Jew's life is only of this world, and his spirit is inwardly as alien to true Christianity as his nature two thousand years previous was to the great founder of the new doctrine".

Thus did Christ make no secret of his attitude toward the Jewish people,

"And when necessary he even took to the whip to drive from the temple of the Lord this adversary of all humanity, who then as always saw in religion nothing but an instrument for his business existence. In return, Christ was nailed to the cross" (66).

National Socialism tried to reconcile neo-paganism with an Aryanised version of Christianity based on the original teachings of the Aryan Christ. Thus, Goebbels *says:*

"If Christ were to be restored as he was, perhaps that would be our redemption" (67).

Neo-pagan racist mystics like Lanz von Liebenfels thus believed that Christ was Aryan. Their "Ario-Christian" doctrine celebrated *"a lost proto-Aryan world… a strange prehistoric world of Godlike Aryan supermen"*, in which Frauja (a Gothic name for Jesus), the saviour of the Aryans, or "forces of light", calls for the sacrifical extermination of the forces of darkness, *the "sub-men, the 'apelings' and all other inferiors"* (68). These mystics truly believed in the pagan Aryan origins of Christianity, whose very name they claimed was Aryan: *"the word 'crystal' (Kristall) was derived from Krist–All, thus indicating an ancient Krist religion of Atlantean and Aryan provenance which had been supposedly bowdlerised as the new religion of Jesus"* (69). The Swastika itself was considered an "Ario-Christian" symbol.

The Aryan concept of the "Inner Christ", or God-Man, versus transcendental Judaeo-Christianity

"Jesus… had denied any chasm between God and Man… the kingdom of God does not come chronologically-historically: it is an "inward change in the individual" \ (ask ? you will recieve) —innate relating   Friedrich Nietzsche

"We need a religion for free men who know and feel that God is within them"

Alfred Rosenberg

The condemnation of Judaeo-Christianity by Nietzsche and later by Nazism is mainly due to its purposive misinterpretation and distortion of Jesus' original message of the "kingdom of heaven within us", or the "Inner Christ" of the esoteric doctrine; that is, the purely supra-historical, spiritual doctrine of Esoteric Christianity as opposed to the historical and dogmatic doctrine of exoteric Christianity and the latter's concept of the "kingdom of heaven in the Beyond", i.e. its belief in a transcendent unreachable God, as shown in Nietzsche's following passage:

> "Jesus had done away with the concept 'guilt' itself- he had denied any chasm between God and man, he lived this unity of God and man as his 'glad tidings'..." (70). "What did Christ deny? Everything that is today called Christian... precisely that which is Christian in the ecclesiastical sense is anti-Christian in essence: things and people instead of symbols; history instead of eternal facts; forms, rites, dogmas instead of a way of life. Utter indifference to dogmas, cults, priests, church, theology is Christian... Jesus starts directly with the condition the 'kingdom of Heaven' is in the heart, and he does not find the means to it in the observances of the Jewish church; the reality of Judaism itself he regards as nothing; he is purely inward- He likewise ignores the entire system of crude formalities governing intercourse with God: he opposes the whole teaching of repentance and atonement; he demonstrates how one must live in order to feel 'deified'- and how one will not achieve it through repentance and contrition for one's sins: 'sin is of no account' is his central judgment... The Kingdom of Heaven is a condition of the heart... not something 'above the earth'. The Kingdom of God does not 'come' chronologically-historically, on a certain day in the calendar, something that might be here one day but not the day before: it is an 'inward change in the individual', something that comes at every moment and at every moment has not yet arrived" (71).

Nietzsche goes further in his explanation of his concept of the "inner Christ" (which is, as we have already pointed out, an Aryan mystical interpretation of Christianity), by explaining that Jesus was a *"great symbolist"* who *"took for realities, for 'truths', only inner realities- that he understood the rest, everything pertaining to nature, time, space, history, only as signs, as occasion for metaphor"...* Nietzsche indeed believed that nothing was more un-Christian than the "ecclesiastical crudities" of a God as a person, of a "kingdom of Heaven" in the Beyond, of a "Son of God", and that the "kingdom of God" was "not something one waits for", rather it is an inner experience which this "bringer of glad tidings" sought to share with the world, dying *"as he lived, as he taught- not to 'redeem mankind' but*

[handwritten margin note: misreading of the bible]

to demonstrate how one ought to live. What he bequeathed to mankind is his practice" (72). Christ's essential teaching and his concept of the "Son of God" was *therefore "not a dogma or a cult, but a way of life which he practised as a means to inward peace"* (73).

It is the Church's distortion of this original message (in order to subjugate the masses by inculcating the notions of submissiveness and humility into their minds) from an inner state and experience into a transcendental "Heaven above us", which heralds Christianity's break with Jesus' original teaching. Thus spoke Nietzsche:

> *"To resume, I shall now relate the real history of Christianity.- The word 'Christianity' is already a misunderstanding- in reality there has been only one Christian, and he died on the Cross. The 'Evangel' died on the Cross. What was called 'Evangel' from this moment onwards was already the opposite of what he had lived: 'bad tidings', a dysangel... Only Christian practice, a life such as he who died on the Cross lived, is Christian... Even today, such a life is possible, for certain men even necessary: genuine, primitive Christianity will be possible at all times.... Not a belief but a doing, above all a not-doing of many things, a different being ..." (74).*

not a faith - but a way of life

In short, for Nietzsche (as for Aryan pagan mysticism), Christianity was an inner experience, a practice, and not an outer "truth"... Therefore, true Christianity does not come from blind adherence to a limited set of ideas ("God", "the Beyond", "Heaven", ...), what Nietzsche termed "crude answers", but from a direct personal encounter with the spiritual reality, with the "God within".

Adopting Nietzsche's views on Christ and Christianity, the Nazis also believed that true Christianity was based on the mystical concept *"the kingdom of heaven within us"*, and Chamberlain, basing himself on Christ's own words: *"the Kingdom of God cometh not with observation: neither shall they say, Lo here or lo there. For behold, the Kingdom of God is within you"* (75), acknowledges this concept of an inner Christ:

> *"These words of Christ have, however, as we can see, never the character of a doctrine... Down through the ages we hear the words, 'Learn of me,' and we understand what they mean: to be as Christ was, to live as Christ lived, to die as Christ died, that is the Kingdom of God, that is eternal life" (76).*

As for Rosenberg, Nazi Germany's official philosopher, he derived from the mediaeval mystic Meister Eckhart, the belief that in the true religious experience, the soul meets God *"at the ground of one's being"*, which he asserted was *"the blood"* (77), i.e. man's inmost spiritual being, his Higher Self, as opposed to Christianity's "God in heaven":

"Rosenberg's 'religion of the blood' is not based upon dogmatic creeds, alleged historical events and hollow ceremonies, like Christianity, but upon the experiential certainty of the mystical experience".

Consequently, Rosenberg affirms:

"One is either a German or a Christian. You cannot be both... We need free men who feel and know that God is in themselves... The Ten Commandments have lost their validity... Our peasants have not forgotten their true religion. It still lives... The peasant will be told what the Church has destroyed for him: the whole secret knowledge of nature, of the divine, the shapeless, the daemonic... We shall wash off the Christian veneer and bring out a religion peculiar to our race...through the peasantry we shall really be able to destroy Christianity because there is in them a true religion rooted in nature and blood" (78).

Rosenberg believed that the church had stolen from the German peasant -in whom lay the hope for a spiritual rebirth -for the peasant is in a mystical communion with nature- the mysterious and direct link with nature, the instinctive contact, the communion with the *"spirit of the earth"*. Therefore he and Hitler rejected the *"servile Judaeo-Christian religion of weakness and pity"*, advocating the belief in a stronger heroic faith, a belief in God which would be inseparable from the Aryan's destiny and his blood, a faith that does not reject and negate this life in favour of a life in the "beyond", an Aryan religion for free men, who, in Alfred Rosenberg's own words, *"know and feel that God is within them"*. For Nietzsche and the Nazis, therefore, the pagan Aryan notions of the *"inner Christ"* and *"the kingdom of God within us"* were contrasted with Semitic Judaeo-Christianity's notions of the *"historical Christ"* and the transcendent *"kingdom of God above us"*... Also, Nietzsche and Nazism both called for a return to nature, praising its "cruelty" as the embodiment of the Will to Power as life principle, and despising modern man who is *"afraid to look nature in the face"*, the fact which undeniably makes them true pagans.

CHAPTER THREE

THE WILL TO POWER AS LIFE PRINCIPLE:

A MORALITY BEYOND GOOD AND EVIL

Hitler does quote Nietzsche but does not mean he was a direct influence

"*Life is will to power... where I found a living creature, there I found will to power... willing in general is nothing else but willing to become stronger, willing to grow– and also willing the means thereto*"

Friedrich Nietzsche

"*Life is will to power... he who wants to live must fight and he who does not want to fight in this world of eternal struggle, does not deserve to be alive*"

Adolf Hitler

"Life is Will to Power (1)... Where I found a living creature, there I found Will to Power; and even in the will of the servant I found the will to be master" (2): by adopting the concept of the Will to Power as his philosophy of life, which culminates in the creation of the Superman, Nietzsche becomes the posthumous prophet of Nazism, an ideology whose essence rests in its veneration of spiritual and physical power, incarnated in the Aryan Superman.

The "Will to Power": no other words best describe or summarise- in a nutshell - Nietzsche's philosophy... and the Nazi ideology (and practice...). In fact, for Nietzsche -and later for the Nazis, the whole universe is made up of the Will to Power, and value consists of a morality of force and energy:

> *"There is nothing to life that has value, except the degree of power - assuming that life itself is the Will to Power... All 'purposes', 'goals', 'meanings' [Sinne] are only modes of expression and transformations of the one will inherent in all happenings: the Will to Power... Willing in general is nothing else but willing to become stronger, willing to grow- and also willing the means thereto"* (3).

> *Hitler's life was indeed the perfect manifestation of the Will to Power, for, as Allan Bullock reminds us: "no word was more frequently on Hitler's lips than 'Will', and his whole career from 1919 to 1945 is a remarkable achievement of willpower"* (4).

Hence, for both the Nietzschean and Nazi doctrines, the Will to Power, the *"unexhausted, procreating life-will"* (5), is a philosophy of life, a global vision of the world, the life principle (i.e. the origin, essence and purpose of life), the motor of history, and the origin of morality... In short, it is *the* supreme truth, in fact, the *only* truth. As such, it is in direct opposition and transcends both the contemplative "will to truth" and the liberal-positivist "will to life" or self-preservation. According to the radically elitist Nietzschean and Nazi doctrines, *true* justice speaks thus: Might makes Right; Life is a struggle, and its purpose lies in the struggle itself, the latter being a creative process of spiritual purification... Only the fittest, the strongest survive in this cruel world, whereas the weak and degenerate beings are trampled upon by the superior species: that is to the iron aristocratic law of nature praised by Nietzsche and Hitler.

It is worth noting in this respect that what Nietzsche means by "power" goes far beyond mere political power, and should be understood as absolute,

global power: i.e. physical, spiritual, moral, mental, *and* political power …
And this absolute power is exactly what the Nazis sought to attain through
their racial policies aimed at breeding an Aryan Master Race, superior in
body and soul, and through their expansionist military policies aimed at
acquiring *Lebensraum* ("vital space"), i.e. new colonies where they would
enslave 'sub-humans' such as the Slavs and Jews. Furthermore, the Will to
Power is not a striving *after* power as a means, but rather a state of being
man desires for its own sake; for the slave, it is a desire for freedom, and
for the master, the higher man, it is the need to discharge an abundance of
power, it is the will to bestow power.

One can safely venture to say that the Will to Power doctrine,
created by Nietzsche and espoused by the Nazis, is mainly a matter of
overcoming, and has a three-fold dimension: first, it is the overcoming
of Judaeo-Christian morality with its conceptions of good and evil and
its transcendental, personal and distant God, the fact which calls for a
revaluation of values in favour of the Master Morality as opposed to the
currently prevailing Slave Morality. The Will to Power is the origin of
morality, a morality "beyond good and evil" which is immanent in nature;
second, the Will to Power consists of self-overcoming, a spiritual process
which starts with the mastery of our passions and must ultimately lead to
the creation of a higher species of man, the Superman; and third, the Will
to Power also means the overcoming of the weak by the strong; as such, it
is a glorification of struggle, war, domination, and the exploitation of the
weak and unworthy subhuman slaves, by the strong and creative Masters,
the "Lords of the Earth"…

Most scholars view Nietzsche as the prophet of "power politics" -and
hence, I argue, of Nazism- for his veneration of power has definite political
consequences, especially when we consider the particularly significant
circumstances which inspired Nietzsche to "create" the concept of the
Will to Power… Nietzsche's sister thus describes how he came up with
this ingenious idea, which was to become his *Weltanschauung* ("vision of
the world") and the cornerstone of his whole philosophy:

*"He was serving in the hospital corps during the war of 1870. After a
day of fatigue and horror on the battlefield, he suddenly heard a noise like
thunder approaching and fresh Prussian regiments dashed past, eager for
combat. It then occurred to him that life at its best was not a wretched
struggle for existence but a fight for power" (6).*

Given this statement, one cannot but imagine what Nietzsche would have felt had he lived to see the endless columns of iron-disciplined, goose-stepping, black steel-helmeted, ruthless-looking and extremely virile S.S. soldiers parading before his eyes; in short, "the Will to Power on the march"... Indeed, I shall show in this chapter that, if it is an undeniable fact that the concept of the Will to Power was Nietzsche's own brainchild, it is nevertheless also an equally undeniable fact that the S.S., Nazi Germany's Aristocracy, was the living embodiment of this concept in every respect: the Nazi cult which the S.S. venerated thus preached "immoralism" in the Nietzschean sense of a transvaluation of Master and Slave Moralities in favour of the former; Nazism also called for self-overcoming as the bridge to the Superman, a process which involved heavy discipline and hardness towards oneself, a strong sense of sacrifice, unshakable loyalty to one's duty, and obedience to one's superiors; finally, it glorified war as higher life-affirmation and preached the ruthless and cruel domination and exploitation of the born-slaves by the natural aristocrats.

A. The Will to Power as the origin of Morality: a transvaluation of values

1. The death of the transcendent God as Man's great liberation: "beyond good and evil"

"God is dead... The concept 'God' has hitherto been the greatest objection to existence... It was suffering and impotence that created all afterworlds..."

"I entreat you, my brothers, remain true to the earth, and do not believe those who speak to you of superterrestrial hopes! They are poisoners... despisers of life... Once blasphemy against God was the greatest blasphemy, but God died, and thereupon these blasphemers died too. To blaspheme the earth is now the most dreadful offence, and to esteem the bowels of the Inscrutable more highly than the meaning of the earth..."

Friedrich Nietzsche

"If Nazism was a religion, it was a religion which offered no 'other place' to go to... it made no appeal to the supra-material or personal transcendence, the greater good, to God or state. It desired itself... The danger of the Nazi 'revelation' is that it alluded to an imminent or latent power, not to a transcendent one- This immediately abolished the traditional division

between the secular and the sacred, and replaced the 'otherwordly' vision
of religion with a heightened perception of an existing reality"

Malcom Quinn

Author of *The Swastika: Constructing the Symbol*

"God is dead!" Thus spoke Zarathustra, alias Nietzsche, heralding the "twilight of the idols", i.e. the demise of Christian Morality which, by inventing a "Beyond", a life after death, and ascribing perfection *only* to this "hidden world" -while condemning our actual world as "imperfect" and "sinful"- has kept man in mental and moral bondage of a transcendental distant "God" for centuries, thus preventing him from pursuing his highest -in fact, only- attainable aim in life, which is self-perfection and self-overcoming... Indeed, Nietzsche vehemently rejects what has hitherto been called Morality with its notions of "Good" and "Evil" as a symptom of decadence, of declining life, for its conception of a life after death

"has historically furnished the basis for the depreciation of this life. The
expectation of perfection in another world has made men condone their
imperfection in this world. Instead of striving to become perfect here and
now, as Jesus had exhorted them to do, they put their trust in the distant
future" (7).

For Nietzsche, *"it was suffering and impotence- that created all afterworlds*
(8)... the concept 'God' invented as the antithetical concept to life. The concept
'the Beyond', 'real world' invented so as to deprive of value the only world which
exists- so as to leave over no goal, no reason, no task for our earthly reality!" (9).
Therefore, it is only through the elimination of the transcendental concept of "God" as an external abstract notion alien to man's life and purpose in *this* world, that we can hope to restore human greatness, a greatness which prevailed in ancient pre-Christian pagan times, before the invention of morality... Only thus would Christian Morality, "the denial of life", cease to be "an aim of life, an aim of evolution", as has hitherto been the case, for *"our greatest reproach against existence was the existence of God"* (10). In other words, the "death of God" is Man's great liberation, for only by "killing" *this* external concept can humanity aspire to earthly perfection.

This virulent rejection of the Judaeo-Christian transcendental and personal God (in contrast to Christ's original message of the "Kingdom of Heaven within us" -i.e. the theosophical concept of the "inner Christ"), so characteristic of Nietzsche, was also a prominent feature of the Nazi ideology. Indeed, Alfred Rosenberg, Nazi Germany's official philosopher, clearly reflects, in his major work, *The Myth of the Twentieth Century*, Nazism's firm rejection of the Judaeo-Christian notion of

"a God who made the world out of nothing, and who intervenes in its course to perform miracles. He insists that the Germanic soul recognizes a reign of law in the world of phenomena. He rejects a God whose commands are arbitrary, who demands humility, who delegates to priests a power of giving or withholding salvation. The inner spiritual world is also a realm of law" (11).

It is worth noting that both Nietzsche's and Nazism's "atheism" is effectively a moral, spiritual, and even religious position deriving from their pagan conception of divinity as immanent in nature. Their refusal to believe in *a* transcendental god in no sense denies that God nonetheless *does* exist (but is immanent and reachable), and that human life in itself is worthy and perfectible, in contrast to the conventional atheistic attitude which is materialistic in character. In fact, Nietzsche and the Nazis were pagans, *not* atheists (the difference is great), that is, they believed in God, yet this belief was pantheistic and internal (i.e. mystical), not transcendental and external; Nietzsche clearly shows us in his *Zarathustra* that he does believe in *some* God, *his own* God, rejecting the "old" God, i.e. the traditional conception of a "God in heaven":

"Away with such a god! Better no god, better to produce destiny on one's own account, better to be God oneself! O Zarathustra, you are more pious than you believe, with such an unbelief! Some god in you has converted you to your godlessness. Is it not your piety itself that no longer allows you to believe in a god? This old god no longer lives: he is quite dead" (12).

The fact is that man *can* and *should* be overcome, but this overcoming is due to his own free will; man is absolutely free to pursue his own self-perfection, no one else is accountable for his success or failure, as Nietzsche's following passage in *Twilight of the Idols* best illustrates:

"What alone can our teaching be? - That no one gives a human being his qualities: not God, not society, not his parents or ancestor, not he himself... One is necessary, one is a piece of fate, one belongs to the whole, one is in the whole- there exists nothing which could judge, measure, compare, condemn our being, for that would be to judge, measure, compare, condemn the whole... But nothing exists apart from the whole! - That no one is any longer made accountable... this alone is the great liberation- thus alone is the innocence of becoming restored... The concept 'God' has hitherto been

the greatest objection to existence... We deny God; in denying God, we deny accountability: only by doing that do we redeem the world.-" (13).

Similarly, for Nazism, there is no such thing as an 'absolute' and 'ultimate' truth revealed 'from above', a truth which would be the same for everyone, rather several 'truths' according to one's race and purpose; Rosenberg thus

"rejects the Hellenic search for absolute, all-inclusive truth, which still dominates philosophy. An organic living creature possesses 'form' (Gestalt); its inner and outer structure is adapted to purpose; and its mental and spiritual life pursues goals... He considers it utterly perverse to seek through mere cognition an absolute and eternal truth identical for all mankind, because truth is relative to the organic life of the essentially unchangeable race. 'The ultimate insight possible to a race is already implicit in its first religious myth' " (14).

The Will to Power is the *sole* truth, for it is the only humanly palpable, humanly conceivable truth, i.e. the only immanent reality *and* purpose which man should seek, for it guarantees creativity; thus does Nietzsche preach:

"Willing liberates: that is the true doctrine of will and freedom- thus Zarathustra teaches you. No more to will and no more to evaluate and no more to create! ah, that this great lassitude may ever stay far from me!... This will lured me away from God and gods; for what would there be to create if gods- existed!" (15).

To will is therefore an act of creation; through his Will to Power, man becomes the centre of the universe, thus transcending his finite existence.

"Shatter, you enlightened men, shatter the old law-tables!" (16): by condemning Morality, Nietzsche is announcing the advent of nihilism, which has become necessary "because the values we have had hitherto thus draw their final consequence... We require, sometime, new values" (17). However, the nihilism he is preaching is an "active nihilism", i.e. "nihilism as a sign of increased power" which he contrasts with passive nihilism, i.e. "nihilism as decline and recession of the power of the spirit" (18). Therefore, his destruction of old values is in itself a creative work, for it aims at establishing new, higher values:

"He who has to be a creator in good and evil, truly, has first to be a destroyer and break values. Thus the greatest evil belongs with the greatest good: this, however, is the creative good" (19).

Nietzsche's "active nihilism" was also a prevalent feature of Nazism, whose advent heralded a spiritual-pagan 'New Age' aimed at creating a higher species of man, shattering the very foundations of Liberal Western Civilisation, i.e. the Judaeo-Christian tradition and its old standards of evaluation which have ruled humanity for nearly two thousand years... Hitler indeed proclaimed that he was humanity's 'great liberator' who would free mankind from the 'illusion' called 'conscience' or 'Morality', preaching a new moral freedom which only true 'free spirits' could endure...

Active Nihilism, for both Nietzsche and the Nazis, thus meant the "self-overcoming of morality", because *"Morality itself, in the form of honesty, compels us to deny morality"* (20). Yet nihilism was only the first step in the establishment of new values, of a new philosophy "beyond Good and Evil"; in this light, Nietzsche's Zarathustra, who preached the overcoming of Morality's conceptions of Good and Evil, can only be viewed as an attempt to "correct" or transcend the dualism of the historical Zarathustra (the Persian prophet whose worldview was based on the eternal conflict between the powers of light and the powers of darkness), a dualism which was also to form a basic tenet of the Christian faith, one of the main reasons Nietzsche rejected Christianity.

By postulating the Will to Power as the origin of morality and only reality, the Nietzschean and Nazi ideologies were drawn to the following logical consequence: "God" and Morality are dead, and with them the *"old delusion called Good and Evil"* (21). Therefore, without the promise of eternal bliss in the "Beyond" which would be life's final purpose, there can be no ultimate right or wrong, no "good" or "evil", for life has no purpose but itself: *"There are neither moral nor immoral actions (22)... there are no opposites... everything has become: there are no eternal facts, just as there are no absolute truths"* (23). Nothing has been created, everything is eternally becoming; Becoming is the only reality, the creative force and the inexorable law of the universe. Hitler clearly had in mind Nietzsche's concept of Will to Power when he confided in Rauschning that Man sought action for its own sake, that life itself was nothing but confrontation, tension of the will, perpetual overcoming, and that anything which is limited, finite, or static is inexorably destined to die...

When Hermann Goering proclaimed: "I have no conscience: my conscience is called Adolf Hitler", he was practicing the "great, cold absence of prejudices" which the Fuehrer had always demanded of his followers, an attitude in accordance with the morality "beyond good and evil" which Nazism preached in words and deeds... a morality which rested on an entirely different set of values than the commonly accepted notions of good and evil... In Nazi Germany there reigned, for a few years, a civilisation radically different from the liberal-humanist civilisation; the following passage well illustrates the Nazi phenomenon's uniqueness in terms of "supra-moral" values:

"Certain sessions of the Nuremberg Trial were meaningless. The judges could not possibly have any kind of communication with those who were really responsible... Two worlds confronted one another, with no means of communication. It was like trying to judge creatures from Mars by the standards of our humanist civilization. They were, indeed, Martians- in the sense that they belonged to a different world from the one we have known for the last six or seven centuries. A civilization totally different from what is generally meant by the word had been established in Germany in the space of a few years, without our having ever properly understood what was going on. Its initiators no longer had any intellectual, moral or spiritual affinities with ourselves in any basic sense.... despite external resemblances... The judges at Nuremberg tried to act as if they were not conscious of this appalling state of things" (24).

Only by overcoming morality through the adoption of a philosophy "beyond good and evil", beyond the eternal dualism between good and evil, body and spirit, which characterises the transcendentalist vision of the world, would we be able to restore the "innocence of becoming", i.e. to live in accordance with nature, "in the here and now, for the here and now" (25); both Nietzsche and the Nazis were in fact staunchly "immanentist": they believed in human perfection in the *actual* world, opposing both transcendentalism (the "will to truth") and materialism (the "will to life"), for the former's 'flight from reality' denied perfection in *this* life, i.e. denied Life, while the latter denied the very possibility of perfection, reducing human life to a mere desire for self-preservation and search for material comfort, i.e. the reign of mediocrity... In short, both transcendentalism and materialism denied the Will to Power as life-principle and only *immanent* truth which manifests itself in all aspects of life.

The actual world is the *only* real world, and *"it could be that the other world is the 'apparent' one"* (26); therefore, *this* world is the only one which has value, for its spiritual and physical dimensions are both manifestations of the *sole* life-affirming principle: the Will to Power. Against transcendentalism, Nietzsche reproaches its "will to truth" to be a principle that is "hostile to life and destructive", urging the "Higher Men" to *"remain true to the earth"* and not to believe *"those who speak to you of superterrestrial hopes!"*, for *"they are poisoners... despisers of life.* For Nietzsche,

> *"once blasphemy against God was the greatest blasphemy, but God died, and thereupon these blasphemers died too. To blaspheme the earth is now the most dreadful offence, and to esteem the bowels of the Inscrutable more highly than the meaning of the earth" (27).*

Nazism also sought spiritual and racial perfection in Nietzsche's "Kingdom of Earth", rejecting any "reality" in the "Beyond", and affirming instead, in Hitler's words: "In the beginning was action"... The only thing that mattered was action, not the search for a transcendent 'truth', for action itself was the key to understanding and becoming conscious of the essence of the universe. Indeed,

> *"if Nazism was a religion, it was a religion which offered no 'other place' to go to. In Nazi propaganda, the racial purge through which the German becomes the Germanic is ideologically accomplished in a 'future state' which is constructed, paradoxically, as a return to a pre-existing truth. The Nazi idea was not simply metaphysical, but ontological",*

This fact may account for the descriptive summary of Nazism as *"the practical and violent "resistance to transcendence"* :

> *Nazism was not an ideology in the traditional sense, since it made no appeal to the supra-material or personal transcendence, the greater good, to God or state. It desired itself... racism does not 'legitimise' power so much as 'establish' it... The rights of 'better blood' rendered civil rights null and void. The danger of the Nazi 'revelation' was that it alluded to an immanent or latent power, not to a transcendent one. This immediately abolished the traditional division between the secular and the sacred, and replaced the 'otherwordly' vision of religion with a heightened perception of an existing reality through communal experience" (28).*

However, the Nietzschean and Nazi doctrines' firm condemnation of transcendentalism certainly does not make them Cartesian rationalists...

On the contrary, Nietzsche took equal pride in proclaiming himself the *"strongest opponent of all materialism"* (29), showing only contempt for the latter's faith in the evidence of the senses as a source of ultimate certitude, and considering that reason never supplies the impetus for human action:

> *"Against positivism, which halts at phenomena- 'There are only facts'- I would say: No, facts are precisely what they are not, only interpretations."* *(30).*

Thoroughly denouncing the entire rationalist tradition of the Enlightenment and the moral vacuum it has left behind, Nietzsche scorned the liberal-humanist principle of the "will to Life" as a mere desire for self-preservation (in direct opposition to the life-affirming creative Will to Power), the uncreative drive of the mediocre, common "herd animal" who seeks "happiness" instead of power:

> *"For what do the trees in a jungle fight each other? For 'happiness"?- For power!"* *(31).*

Power is the essence of life, and therefore, the search for mere survival and happiness is nothing but a delusion:

> *"He who shot the doctrine of 'will to existence' at truth certainly did not hit the truth: this will - does not exist! .... Only where life is, there is also will: not will to life, but -so I teach you - Will to Power!"* *(32).*

The Nazi ideology's immanentist-ontological vision of the world also led it to oppose Enlightenment Rationalism, considering its belief that only through reason and 'objective science' can man discover the secrets of the universe, as a mere delusion and false reality. As Hitler confided to Rauschning, we are witnessing the end of the era of reason and the advent of a new era where will, not knowledge, will explain the mysteries of the universe. Intuition and "Magic" (i.e. the spiritual worldview) was to replace Reason, for *"Cartesian reason does not cover the whole of Man and the whole of his knowledge"*... Nazism transcended Reason and the latter, *"pushed to its extreme limits, was operating on a higher level, linking up with the mysteries of the mind and spirit, the secrets of energy and universal harmony"* (33).

Thus, for both Nietzsche and the Nazis, reality was neither good nor evil, neither spirit nor matter, but rather, the unity of these notions: *"One should write of the unity of good and evil, the inseparability of the one from the other, make good more attractive by giving it violent and exciting company"* (34), wrote Nietzsche. Stressing the organic and fundamental unity of all of nature, both doctrines aspired to totality, striving against the separation of mind and body, in order to attain perfection symbolised by the union between the Apollonian and Dionysian spirits...

"A healthy mind in a healthy body"... Nowhere does this axiom find more credence than in the philosophies of Nietzsche and National Socialism: indeed, while Nietzsche scorns the soul which "looks contemptuously upon the body" as well as the "weak, sickly body" which pretends to possess a "sublime soul", Hitler echoes this rejection of the mind-spirit duality by asserting that

"a healthy, forceful spirit will be found only in a healthy and forceful body... A decayed body is not made the least more aesthetic by a brilliant mind, indeed the highest intellectual training could not be justified if its bearers were at the same time physically degenerate and crippled, weak-willed, wavering and cowardly individuals".

For the Fuehrer, as for Nietzsche, true perfection is always both spiritual and physical:

"What makes the Greek ideal of beauty a model is the wonderful combination of the most magnificent physical beauty with the brilliant mind and the noblest soul" (35).

Against Being, or static truth, Nietzsche and the Nazis oppose Becoming, i.e. a dynamic, ever-changing, eternally creative and unending process, without a final purpose. Everything is in a perpetual flux, an endless becoming, therefore the search for a final purpose (Being) is pointless. Best represented by Nietzsche's doctrine of the Eternal Recurrence and the Nazi Swastika (which symbolises perpetual creation), the concept of Becoming is but one of the manifestations of the Will to Power... as illustrated by Nietzsche's following description of the "World":

"And do you know what 'the world' is to me? Shall I show it to you in my mirror? This world: a monster of energy, without beginning, without end..... as force throughout... a sea of forces flowing and rushing together, eternally changing, eternally flooding back, with tremendous years of recurrence, with an ebb and a flood of its forms.... blessing itself as that which must return eternally, as a becoming that knows no satiety, no disgust, no weariness: this, my Dionysian world of the eternally self-creating, the eternally self-destroying, this mystery world of the twofold voluptuous delight, my 'beyond good and evil'.... This world is the Will to Power- and nothing besides! And you yourselves are also this Will to

Power- and nothing besides!" (36).

2. Immoralism as a transvaluation of values: Master Morality versus Slave Morality

"Life is the struggle of the many against the few, the commonplace against the rare, the weak against the strong"

Friedrich Nietzsche

"World history is made by minorities… it is never the masses or the majority who create but always the individual… Superior and talented men should be in control"

Adolf Hitler

"Can all values be turned round? And is good perhaps evil?"

"Jesus said to his Jews: 'the law was made for servants- love God as I love him, as his son! What have we sons of God to do with morality!"

" 'Equal to the equal, unequal to the unequal'- that would be the true slogan of justice"

Friedrich Nietzsche

"The SS man must have contempt for all racial inferiors and for those who do not belong to the Order; he must feel the strongest bonds of comradeship with those who do belong, particularly his fellow soldiers, and he must think nothing impossible"

SS Creed of Combat

"They do not understand me, I am not the mouth for these ears" (37): Zarathustra's greatest mistake, according to Nietzsche, was to preach his radically elitist philosophy "beyond good and evil" to the common herd of the market-place, a 'lower humanity' unable to understand such deep thoughts… Therefore, he chose henceforth to direct his highest teachings to the 'very few', i.e. Higher Men who had the courage to accept life's true essence and purpose, which was none other than the Will to Power. Similarly, the Nazis believed that only a certain racial and spiritual elite was equipped to grasp life's deepest secrets. Truth was a matter of courage, and only a few superior beings could bear to look reality in the face and to live according to the aristocratic law of nature.

In fact, all aristocratic, non-egalitarian, hierarchically ordered civilisations distinguish between common exoteric knowledge available to all men, and esoteric knowledge, reserved for the elect few. As Nietzsche states,

> *"our supreme insights must- and should!- sound like follies, in certain cases like crimes, when they come impermissible to the ears of those who are not predisposed and predestined for them. The exoteric and the esoteric as philosophers formerly distinguished them, among the Indians as among the Greeks, Persians and Moslems, in short wherever one believed in an order of rank and not in equality and equal rights" (38).*

By declaring that *"world history is made by minorities"* (39), Adolf Hitler, whose doctrine rejects the democratic majority-principle and rests instead on the *Fuehrersprinzip* or "leadership principle", proves himself a true Nietzschean, for Nietzsche saw life mainly as *"the struggle of the many against the few, the commonplace against the rare, the weak against the strong"* (40). For Hitler, too, it is never the masses or the majority who create, but always the exceptional individual, the Higher Man; therefore, to ensure progress, the best elements of the community should be given the reins of power...

The logical inference Nietzsche and the Nazis drew from this sharp dualism between minority and majority, between the few and the many, is the following: humanity is not "one", as humanists, Liberals and Socialists alike, maintain; rather, it is divided into two distinct and unequal 'species' of man, the (rare) Masters and the (numerous) slaves; consequently, morality and justice are neither universal nor absolute...

In this respect, Nietzsche affirms that *"one should defend virtue against the preachers of virtue: they are its worst enemies. For they teach virtue as an ideal for everyone; they take from virtue the charm of rareness, inimitableness, exceptionalness and unaverageness- its aristocratic magic"* (41), despising the English Utilitarians, a modest and "thoroughly mediocre" species of man, for their unwillingness to acknowledge the fact that virtue is *not* universal, that *"the demand for one morality for all is detrimental to precisely the higher men, in short that there exists an order of rank between man and man, consequently also between morality and morality"* (42). As for Alfred Rosenberg, he *"scorns the idea of universal truth. What he claims to present is the essential truth for Nordics, and especially Germans, in the twentieth century"* (43). Justice should thus not be considered an *"abstract idea applicable to men as such regardless of race"* (44).

Indeed, a characteristic feature of the Nietzschean and Nazi doctrines is their opposition to the notion that *all* human beings have both a moral dignity and moral rights: true justice is unequal, since, as Nietzsche states,

"those born without noble souls have little to develop into… 'Become who you are:' that is a call that is only ever allowed for the few, but for the very few is superfluous"… (45).

Therefore, Nietzsche pursues, *"he has discovered himself who says: This is my good and evil: he has silenced thereby the mole and dwarf who says: 'Good for all, evil for all' "* (46).

Since Justice and Morality are not universal, it follows that there is a hierarchy of values and, consequently, two different -indeed, antithetical- moralities, what Nietzsche termed *"master morality and slave morality"* (47), the former characterised by pride, honour, and glory, the latter by envy and resentment. In line with their radically aristocratic view of the world, the Nietzschean and Nazi doctrines divide humanity into superhuman "Masters" and subhuman "slaves", each having their own set of values. For Nietzsche, the Master views the antithesis 'good' and 'bad' as identical to 'noble' and 'despicable', the antithesis 'good' and 'evil' originating elsewhere (48):

"Evil actions belong to the powerful and virtuous: bad, base ones to the subjected" (49).

Nietzsche's Master Morality may be summarised as follows:

"The cowardly, the timid, the petty, and those who think only of narrow utility are despised… The noble type of man feels himself to be the determiner of values … he creates values. Everything he knows to be part of himself, he honours: such a morality is self-glorification. In the foreground stands the feeling of plenitude, of power which seeks to overflow, the happiness of high tension, the consciousness of a wealth which would like to give away and bestow- the noble human being too aids the unfortunate but not, or almost not, from pity, but from an urge begotten by superfluity of power" (50).

Despising the Christian 'slavish' virtues of the "warm heart", "selflessness", and "disinterest", the Master shows an inborn natural dignity of high rank and a reverence for the past and tradition, together with contempt for "modern" egalitarian ideas of "progress".

This Nietzschean highly aristocratic morality justifies arbitrary conduct and ruthlessness toward the "lower order", namely all those who are alien and inferior, but it has a privilege in its duty toward one's self and one's peers only; that is, equality, duty and loyalty exist only "among equals", i.e. among aristocrats: Nietzsche indeed had the firm conviction that

"one has duties only to one's equals, toward the others one acts as one thinks best: that justice can be hoped for (unfortunately not counted on) only inter pares [among equals]" (51)... 'Equal to the equal, unequal to the unequal'- that would be the true slogan of justice" (52).

Quite significantly, the ideology and code of conduct of the very aristocratic S.S. were astonishingly identical to Nietzsche's Master morality; in fact, it was as if the S.S. had literally adopted this morality as their very own: the S.S. motto, *"Meine Ehre heisst Treue"* ("My Honour is loyalty"), symbolising the spirit of obedience, loyalty, duty and comradeship within the elitist Black Order, testifies to this certainty. The S.S.'s very rigorous standards of selection imposed on their volunteers and their espousal of the following particularly demanding creed of combat, remind us of Nietzsche's eclectic and radically aristocratic values:

"The SS man's basic attitude must be that of a fighter for fighting's sake; he must be unquestioningly obedient and become emotionally hard; he must have contempt for all 'racial inferiors' and for those who do not belong to the order; he must feel the strongest bonds of comradeship with those who do belong, particularly his fellow soldiers, and he must think nothing impossible" (53).

It was in short, a Superman's creed, and Nietzsche would definitely have endorsed it and would have recognised in the S.S. soldier the living embodiment of the Superman to whom he gave theoretical existence...

In sharp contrast to the Master Morality, the Slave Morality is a creation of resentment against the strong, against the Masters. It builds its opposing values of "good and evil" as a reaction to the Master's opposition "good and bad"; it considers the Noble's notion of "good" as "evil", while it endorses the Master's conception of "bad" as its highest "good"... Nietzsche thus highlights the main feature of this 'decadent' morality, the morality of the *"abused, oppressed, suffering, unfree, those uncertain of themselves and weary"*:

"...a pessimistic mistrust of the entire situation of man... The slave is

suspicious of the virtues of the powerful: he is sceptical and mistrustful, keenly mistrustful, of everything 'good' that is honoured among them... On the other hand ... pity, the kind and helping hand, the warm heart, patience, industriousness, humility, friendliness come into honour... Slave morality is essentially the morality of utility. Here is the source of the famous antithesis 'good' and 'evil'- power and danger were felt to exist in evil... Thus, according to slave morality the 'evil' inspire fear; according to master morality it is precisely the 'good' who inspire fear and want to inspire it, while the 'bad' man is judged contemptible... Wherever slave morality comes to predominate, language exhibits a tendency to bring the words 'good' and 'stupid' closer to each other" (54).

In short, the slave morality is a reaction of the weak, the wretched and the world-weary against the strong, healthy aristocratic types; it belongs to the "herd animals" who are "levellers", for their values relax life to an average, mediocre performance...

For the Nazis, this slavish morality was best embodied by the "subhuman" Jew -the perfect antithesis to the Superman-, while the superior Aryan represented the Master morality to perfection. According to Nazi ideology, world history was characterised by the eternal conflict between the antithetical Aryan and Semitic (especially Jewish) spirits or moralities, a clash of civilisations best represented by the conflict between Rome and Judea. When we consider that Nietzsche used the conflict *"Rome against Judea, Judea against Rome"* (55) as his best illustration for the Master-Slave conflict, as the best symbol of the fight between the two antagonistic values of "good and bad", "good and evil", i.e. the strong, aristocratic, natural Roman values versus the weak, slavish, unnatural Jewish values, we cannot but infer that the Nazis clearly had Nietzsche in mind when they referred to the Rome-Judea conflict, and that Nietzsche did indeed view the Aryan-Semitic struggle ("Rome against Judea") as a Master-Slave conflict... Nazism's division of the world between Aryan Supermen and Jewish (and other) sub-humans can thus be viewed as an attempt to prove that Nietzsche's Master-Slave conflict was actually an Aryan-Jew struggle, confirming his assertion that there exists a vast gulf between the high-spirited and the ordinary "little" men, "a gulf so deep as to demarcate two distinct species"...

Given the fact that we are now living in the "Era of the Slave" brought about by the victory of the "Slave Morality" over the "Master Morality", i.e. the 'universalisation' of the egalitarian values of democracy and socialism (whose levelling character only produces mediocrity), and given the fact that the distinction between the existing standards of "good" and "evil" is wholly man-made (each class creating its own values, which are antithetical), it follows that the only way to restore human greatness is through the inversion of the notions of "good" and "evil", for they represent the slave's decadent version of the "lie which has hitherto been called truth"... Therefore, after heralding the advent of "active nihilism" as a destructive but liberating philosophy "beyond good and evil", Nietzsche proceeds to preach a "transvaluation of values" or "immoralism", i.e. a return to the Master Morality, to the aristocratic values and notions of "good and bad" which were prevalent among the ancient Romans and Greeks, a strong, proud and noble species of man.

"The good and just call me the destroyer of morals: my story is immoral" (56): Nietzsche's "immoralism" is the free spirits' war against the old values, an affirmative call for a spiritual awakening confirmed by his assertion that "denial and destruction is a condition of affirmation" (57), and is not to be confused with the anarchist's 'amoralism', i.e. a call for "passive nihilism" or the destruction of the old law-tables without creating values anew. "Evil in the service of the (real) good" was indeed a favourite Nietzschean slogan, for he thought that

> *"when a decadence-species of man has risen to the rank of the highest species of man, this can happen only at the expense of its antithetical species, the species of man strong and certain of life. When the herd-animal is resplendent in the glow of the highest virtue, the exceptional man must be devalued to the wicked man. When mendaciousness at any price appropriates the word 'truth' for its perspective, what is actually veracious must be discovered bearing the worst names" (58);*

Therefore, the only way to restore the aristocrat's "good" is to fight against the slave's "good", i.e. to become "evil":

"Can all values not be turned round? and is good perhaps evil? " (59).

"Evil" and "Nazism": two words which are nowadays so frequently and closely associated in the West, that one doesn't have to go to great lengths to defend the widespread idea that the Nazis were, by all Liberal-humanist, Judaeo-Christian standards of evaluation, highly "immoral", whether in their radically racist and elitist ideology which glorified the Will to Power (best manifested in war) as the primary vehicle of history, or in their ruthless attitude towards all *"Untermenschen"* ("sub-humans") such as the Slavs and Jews, who were viewed as nothing more than *"Menschentiere"* ("human beasts") and consequently treated as such.

Seen as the very incarnation of "evil" by modern-day Liberals, the Nazis, as true Nietzscheans, indeed represented the opposite values of the actually prevailing democratic notion of "good", i.e. Nietzsche's "Slave Morality", for they advocated "immoralism" as a revaluation of all Western values, considering that *any* means -whether good or evil- were justified, provided they lead to the creation of the Superman.

For Nietzsche and Nazism, hence, what is "good" is everything that proceeds from -and increases- power, and what is "bad" is everything that is weak: therefore, an action acquires its value not depending on whether it is intrinsically "good" or "evil", but on whether it guarantees and increases power, and hence leads to spiritual progress, to the self-overcoming of the human species... And history shows that great cultures have mostly arisen by means of powerful and "immoral" actions, which are the highest manifestation of the Will to Power principle inherent in nature; therefore, *"the great epochs of our life are the occasions when we gain the courage to rebaptise our evil qualities as our best qualities"* (60)... *man must grow better and more evil"*, teaches Nietzsche, for *"the most evil is necessary to the Superman's strength"* (61). The Nazis couldn't have agreed more with this blunt statement celebrating the Will to Power as a philosophy "beyond good and evil"...

To use force, to exploit the weak, to deny morality, to make or break contracts, etc ... thus becomes permissible for the Higher Man, for -as Nietzsche says- "when nothing is true, everything is permitted":

"He who can command, he who is a master by 'nature', he who comes on the scene forceful in deed and gesture- what has he to do with contracts?"
(62).

In line with this Nietzschean statement is Hitler's avowed decision to *"make any treaty I require... It will never prevent me from doing at any time what I regard as necessary for Germany's interests"* (63)... which explains the Fuehrer's arbitrary signing and violation of treaties, for he considered the latter as nothing but means to fulfil his highest goals, which were also the highest goals of Aryan humanity. According to Nietzsche and Nazism, "immoralism", put in the service of the Superman, was not only justified and permitted, but actually desirable; thus did Nietzsche write:

"Jesus said to his Jews: 'The law was made for servants- love God as I love

him, as his son! What have we sons of God to do with morality!' " (64).

B. The Will to Power as self-overcoming: the Superman

"Life itself told me this secret: 'Behold', it said, 'I am that which must overcome itself again and again"
Friedrich Nietzsche

"Life is will to power, and satisfaction is in eternal self-overcoming"
Adolf Hitler

"I teach you the Superman; man is something that must be overcome"
Friedrich Nietzsche

"The Aryan is the Prometheus of mankind from whose bright forehead the divine spark of genius has sprung at all times"

"Creation is not yet an end... Man has to be passed and surpassed... A new variety of man is beginning to separate out... Man is becoming God... Man is God in the making... Gods and beasts, this is what our world is made of"
Adolf Hitler

"God has died: now we desire - that the Superman shall live" (65)... Nietzsche's "death of God", far from representing the destructive nihilism of a crude materialist, is instead a deeply spiritual event, announced by a true believer in human perfection; indeed, only by repudiating the existence of a transcendent God and the promise of perfection "in the Beyond", can the Higher Man again be resurrected as "Lord and Master" of the earth, as a Superman, a God-Man who symbolises earthly perfection and mankind's new and highest -yet attainable- goal, for man cannot endure life without giving it a meaning: *"if a goal for humanity is still lacking, is there not still lacking - humanity itself?"* (66).

"I teach you the Superman; man is something that should be overcome" (67): by calling for a better humanity, Nietzsche thus becomes the prophet of the Superman as the "meaning of the earth", the projection of the Will to Power, a *"humanly-conceivable, humanly-evident, humanly palpable"* goal (68) that can become reality through man's creative will, and not a mere fanciful supposition:

"God is a supposition... Could you create a god?... Could you conceive a god? So be silent about all gods! But you could surely create the Superman" ... Once you said 'God' when you gazed upon distant seas; but now I have taught you to say 'Superman' ... The beauty of the Superman came to me as a shadow. Ah, my brothers! What are the gods to me now!" (69).

Therefore, to Nietzsche, life's highest purpose and the noblest manifestation of the Will to Power is man's self-overcoming:

"Life itself told me this secret: 'Behold,' it said, 'I am that which must overcome itself again and again" (70).

For Nietzsche, the Superman should rule the earth, for he represents a higher species of man: he is the purest, the strongest, *"the Roman Caesar with Christ's soul"* (71), who embodies human perfection for he combines the conflicting yet ideal elements of the Apollonian and the Dionysian, being *"artist (creator), saint (lover), and philosopher (knower) in one person"* (72). The Superman has an aristocratic view of the world, which consists of a totally different set of values, and is against all that is common and egalitarian. Here, only a small number of people fit into this radically elitist concept of Superman; indeed, self-overcoming, and consequently, the creation of the Superman, is only reserved for a select few, and remains an impossible goal for the vast majority of men who, Nietzsche argues, have no inherent worth... Nietzsche does distinguish between quantity and quality, and is in favour of the latter. Hence, only by dedicating itself to the promotion of a higher species can ordinary humanity give a meaning to life: *"Not 'mankind' but Overman is the goal!"* (73).

With the outbreak of National Socialism in the early 1920s, the Aryan becomes the Higher Man, the best potential candidate to fit Nietzsche's status of Superman and rule the earth, for he is the source of all creativity and greatness in the world: Adolf Hitler thus asserts in *Mein Kampf*, the Nazi bible, that

"all the human culture, all the results of art, science, and technology that we see before us today, are almost exclusively the creative product of the Aryan... He alone was the founder of all higher humanity... He is the Prometheus of mankind from whose bright forehead the divine spark of genius has sprung at all times... If we were to divide mankind into three groups, the founders of culture, the bearers of culture, the destroyers of culture, only the Aryan could be considered as the representative of the first group" (74).

According to Hitler, the Aryan is the best physically and morally: you find in him this *"magnificent alliance of the most splendid physical beauty with the shining spirit and the nobility of the soul"*. This man, conscious of the greatness of his soul, feels supreme pride; the Aryan is the best actually, but that, for the Fuehrer, is not enough: we must create the Superman. Like Nietzsche, Hitler is convinced of the general mediocrity of the human species: therefore, he argues, man must, by a constant effort of creative will and the elimination of all moral barriers, overcome himself to produce a higher humanity, for life is Will to Power, and satisfaction is in eternal self-overcoming... What could be more Nietzschean?

The Nazis sought to create -biologically and morally- Nietzsche's Superman... Hitler's ultimate aim was in fact *"to perform an act of creation, a divine operation, the goal of a biological mutation which would result in an unprecedented exaltation of the human race and the 'apparition of a new race of heroes and demi-gods and god-men' "* (75), and the Aryan was the most eligible candidate to fulfil this divine role... It was from the ranks of the SS, an order apart, a modern Knighthood chosen by different and higher standards than those of the regular army, and inspired by the ideal of the Superman, who was originally *"the God-man and Christ-man"* (76), that the God-Man was supposed to appear... The SS "Superman" was a "God in the making" embodying the mystical motto "as above, so below"... Nazi Occultists, claiming that the Aryans were *"the sons of the sun, the sons of the gods, the supreme manifestation of life"*, held that the word "race" was derived from *rata*, an old Norse term meaning "root", the fact which proves that God and the Aryan race were identical (77)...

The Superman being mankind's highest purpose, the living incarnation of the Will to Power, it follows that life as such (i.e. the Will to Power) is a process of eternal creation, of perpetual self-overcoming... a process which transcends mere self-preservation and self-mastery to mean man's actual self-sacrifice in order to produce something higher than himself, the Superman. Indeed, in contrast to the Lockian-Hobbesian tradition, Nietzsche thinks of the law of life not as "self-preservation" but as "self-overcoming"; instead of the Liberal's question *"how may man still be preserved?"*, Nietzsche asks *"how shall man be overcome?"* (78).

Self-overcoming also involves self-mastery; men are classified according to their ability to control their own weaknesses and desires:

"The most spiritual men, as the strongest, find their happiness where others would find their destruction: in the labyrinth, in hardness against

themselves and others, in experiments. Their joy is self-conquest: asceticism becomes in them nature, need, and instinct" (79).

Man should be the master, not the slave, of his passions, they are his tools for greatness. Yet self-overcoming, for Nietzsche as well as Nazism, transcends self-mastery to mean the spiritual overcoming of the "human-all too human" condition of man, i.e. the creation of "something beyond man": the God-like Superman... This definition goes well beyond Walter Kaufmann's narrow analysis of Nietzsche's notion of self-overcoming as mere self-control, refusing to see in the Superman anything more than "the man who has mastered his passions"...

Creating the Superman is indeed a near-impossible mission reserved for the very few, for it involves self-mastery and a Spartan-like hardness on oneself and on others: *"All praise to what makes hard!"*, said Nietzsche, adding: *"I do not praise the land where butter and honey - flow!"* (80). But most importantly, self-overcoming requires a readiness and willingness -if not a strong desire- to sacrifice oneself for the sake of the holy cause of producing a higher humanity, and herein lies the real test of greatness for Nietzsche:

"I love those... who sacrifice themselves to the earth, that the earth may one day belong to the Superman... I love him who wants to create beyond himself, and thus perishes" (81)...

Only by "going down" does man "go beyond"... Those who make history are the strong distinctive characters with higher ideals and an enormous ability for self-sacrifice for the sake of such ideals... What Nietzsche means by self-overcoming therefore goes far beyond Kaufmann's superficial and narrow definition of "self-mastery"...

Proclaiming the creation of the Aryan Superman as its ultimate aim, National Socialism praised self-overcoming as man's noblest goal, stressing on the need for sacrifice, struggle, success of a sacred yet dangerous mission, man's utmost loyalty to his huge task, ... in order to reach this stage of perfection. Thus spoke Hitler:

"Creation if not yet an end... A new variety of man is beginning to separate out... Man is becoming God... Man is God in the making" (82).

The Fuehrer considered that this new and higher breed of Man was to emerge solely from the Aryan stock, for not only was the Aryan best equipped, spiritually and biologically, to become this Superman or God-Man, but also, in him was most strongly developed *"the first premise for every truly human culture"* (83), namely the sense of self-sacrifice, the self-overcoming will... The Aryan held *"a heroic world-view, inasmuch as [he] sacrificed individual benefit for the good of the whole world"* (84), willingly subordinating his own ego to the life of the community, and, if the hour demands, even sacrificing it (85).

C. The Will to Power as the drive for conquest and domination: war as higher life-affirmation

"The magnitude of a 'progress' is gauged by the greatness of the sacrifice that it requires: humanity as a mass sacrificed to the prosperity of the one stronger species of man- that would be a progress"

Friedrich Nietzsche

"Life is an eternal struggle, a world where one creature feeds on the other and where the death of the weaker implies the life of the stronger... that is the basically aristocratic principle of nature: the victory of the stronger over the weaker as a means to breed life as a whole towards a higher level and as the precondition for all human progress"

Adolf Hitler

"You should love peace as a means to new wars and the short peace more than the long! I do not exhort you to work but to battle. I do not exhort you to peace, but to victory. May your work be a battle, may your peace be a victory! ... You say it is the good cause that hallows every war? I tell you: it is the good war that hallows every cause- war and courage have done more great things than charity"

Friedrich Nietzsche

"The SS man's basic attitude must be that of a fighter for fighting's sake; he must be unquestioningly obedient and become emotionally hard"

SS creed of combat

"Life is a scaffolding by means of which a select sort of being might rise to a higher sort of task and a higher sort of existence"

Friedrich Nietzsche

"The progress of humanity is like climbing an endless ladder; it is impossible to climb higher without first taking the lower steps"

Adolf Hitler

The Will to Power is a matter of overcoming: overcoming morality, overcoming oneself, and overcoming the others... "Power", for Nietzsche, means self-perfection as well as the domination of the weak by the strong; it thus transcends Walter Kaufmann's own narrow definition of Nietzsche's concept of power, which, in his analysis, is nothing else but peaceful, harmless self-perfection... Nietzsche, in fact, explicitly and specifically defined the Will to Power as follows:

"Life itself is essentially appropriation, injury, overpowering of the strange and weaker, suppression, severity, imposition of one's own forms, incorporation and, at the least and mildest, exploitation..... because life is Will to Power" (86).

The aforementioned statement leaves no room whatsoever for controversy over its interpretation: Nietzsche simply and actually meant what he said... So when he affirms that *"society has never regarded virtue as anything else than a means to strength, power and order"* (87), he is equating the Will to Power with domination, conquest, struggle, war, exploitation, cruelty, slavery, and hierarchy...

The Nazis, too, saw in force and power the motive element in history and acted accordingly... Life was nothing else but a drive for conquest and domination, struggle, exploitation, where only the strongest survived -the weak ones being eliminated by it. According to Hitler, all development was struggle, only force ruled; force was the first law. Christian love, compassion and peace had no place in a Nazi's dictionary; the Nazi commandment was:

"When someone smites me on the cheek, I do not turn the other cheek, nor do I put up my fists; I strike with a thunderbolt" (88).

Inherent in Nietzsche's Will to Power theory, which the Nazis espoused, is the justification, or rather the glorification, of war, a pivotal theme in Nietzsche's philosophy:

"You should love peace as a means to new wars and the short peace more than the long! I do not exhort you to work but to battle. I do not exhort you to peace, but to victory. May your work be a battle, may your peace be a victory! ... You say it is the good cause that hallows even war? I tell

you: it is the good war that hallows every cause. War and courage have done more great things than charity" (89).

Nietzsche saw that the future of German culture rested with the sons of Prussian officers, the *Junkers,* showing utter contempt for the principle *"peace and letting other people alone"* and asserting instead that *"to dominate (herrschen) and to help the highest thought to victory"* was the only thing that could interest him in Germany (90). Deeply imbued with Nietzsche's philosophy, Nazism, which was from the beginning a fighting movement, shared his veneration of war as higher life-affirmation, as the highest manifestation of the Will to Power, stressing on struggle, conflict, fighting, discipline, courage, obedience, the holiness of heroism, as shown by the SS motto: *"The SS man's basic attitude must be that of a fighter for fighting's sake"...*

War, Hitler believed, is the natural order of things; it is the great purifier, man's natural state: mankind *"has grown great in eternal struggle"* (91). History is a perpetual and merciless struggle for life. Therefore, to the Fuehrer, *"he who wants to live must fight and he who does not want to fight in this world of eternal struggle, does not deserve to be alive"* (92): that was the aristocratic principle of nature which the SS adopted, wearing with pride the *Totenkopf* ("death's head") as a symbol of their willingness to give and take death unhesitatingly in the holy cause of National Socialism.

The impressive, astonishing show of strength at the Nuremberg rallies, where hundreds of thousands of black steel-helmeted SS soldiers gathered in perfect discipline to prepare for war, in a quasi-religious ceremony in veneration of Mars, the Greek God of War, prompted an observer to make this interesting comment:

"If a modern ritual magician of the utmost expertise had designed a ritual intended to 'invoke Mars' he could not have come up with anything more effective than the ceremonies used at Nuremberg" (93).

Nietzsche would certainly have praised this Nazi glorification of war, for the S.S. soldiers were

"selected by standards of which Nietzsche would have approved, and inspired by the vision of war and of service to the warlike state and leader which he advanced" (94).

Here it is worth noting that "war", for Nietzsche and the Nazis alike, means something higher than aimless bloody fighting; it is rather a "spiritual war", even a "holy war" undertaken for the sake of the noblest mission on earth, namely the breeding of the Superman; thus spoke Nietzsche:

"My brothers in war! Let your love towards life be love towards your highest hope: and let your highest hope be the highest idea of life! ... and it is: Man is something that should be overcome" (95).

It is therefore a teleological war, and the fighter praised by both the Nietzschean and Nazi doctrines is not a simple soldier with no specific cause, as Nietzsche points out when he says: *"I see many soldiers: if only I could see many warriors!"* (96), but rather, a Knight, a noble warrior with a keen sense of order of rank, guided by honour not interest, whose loyalty and obedience stem from his firm belief in his holy cause:

"My brothers in war! If you cannot be saints of knowledge, at least be its warriors. They are the companions and the forerunners of such sainthood" (97).

We are reminded of Plato's noble class of "Guardians", the "knights of knowledge" in charge of protecting the "Good Order" established by the Philosopher-King.

The SS, like Nietzsche's warriors, were no simple soldiers; they were "political soldiers" involved in ideological combat while conquering and colonising "lower races"; they were "fighting monks" engaged in a crusade for the supremacy of the super-human Aryan Master Race... Their sense of loyalty to their sacred mission was legendary, as shown by their motto, "my honour is loyalty"... which closely fits Nietzsche's following commandment to his "brothers in war":

"To rebel- that shows nobility in a slave. Let your nobility show itself in obeying! Let even your commanding be an obeying! To be a good warrior, 'thou shalt' sounds more agreeable than 'I will' " (98).

Thus, according to Nietzsche and the Nazis, any war undertaken in the holy cause of producing a higher humanity was considered a holy war, and the "spiritual warriors" engaged in such a crusade were hence justified in doing whatever they thought necessary to fulfil their sacred mission... Indeed, for Nietzsche, *"The higher and the terrible man necessarily belong together"* (99), being a synthesis between the Superman and the "inhuman": therefore, the acts of such higher creatures could include -in the least- the domination and exploitation -or even the extermination- of the weak "sub-humans", a perfectly natural behaviour that was sanctified by the "aristocratic principle of nature". *Equal to the equal, unequal to the unequal* being the *true* voice of Justice, nature, which found its highest expression in the Will to Power, hence sanctioned human domination, and, accordingly, any attempt to protect the weak or the helpless was considered immoral, because it was un-natural.

Hitler's attraction to Nietzsche's warlike creed was clearly reflected in his own worldview which praised the *"basically aristocratic principle of nature"* of the victory of the stronger over the weaker as a means to *"breed life as a whole towards a higher level"* and as the *"precondition for all human progress"* (100). Hitler, a neo-Darwinist who believed in the natural law of selection, in the "survival of the fittest", saw life as an eternal struggle, *"a world where one creature feeds on the other and where the death of the weaker implies the life of the stronger"* (101)... Yet who was nature's favourite child, the strongest, the fittest, on whom Providence had conferred "the Master's right"? To the Fuehrer and the Nazis, it was none other than the Aryan, the "Prometheus of mankind"; they considered that the Aryans embodied the unique mental, moral, and spiritual hardihood and dynamism found in Nietzsche's Superman, which entitled them to rule over all non-Aryan "lower races", such as the Celts (of Alpine race), the Slavs (of East-Baltic race —an offshoot of the Alpine race), and the typically Semitic Jews... Race superiority was indeed the kernel of the Nazi ideology on which the "New Order" in Europe -and the world- was to be based...

The "Master's right" also entitled him to exploit -i.e. enslave-beings of the "lower order"... Nietzsche and Hitler in fact called for a "new slavery", for they believed that the highest type was possible only through the subjugation of the lower: *"we must accept this cruel sounding truth, that slavery is of the essence of culture"* (102), Nietzsche asserts; the vast multitude of worthless "natural-born slaves" must labour in order that a few masters, "born leaders", may lead an existence devoted to beauty and art, to "the good and the true", to human perfection. For the Nazis, the Jews, Negroes, and Slavs were the "natural-born slaves", the typical *Untermenschen*; they had no right to live except as servants of the culture-creating Aryan Master Race. Indeed, Hitler saw in slavery a precondition for the formation of higher cultures:

"Without this possibility of using lower human beings", *the Aryan would never have been able to take his first steps toward his future culture"* *(103).*

Sowing the seeds of greatness thus involves -if not requires- hardness and even cruelty towards all that is weak and inferior: *"Become hard!"* (104), Nietzsche entreated his "brothers", the Higher Men, praising the proud Viking's "hard heart" which rejected the *"great nausea with man... the great pity for man"* (105)... Cruelty is necessary for producing "something higher than man", a task which, according to Nietzsche, requires the elimination of everything that impedes the progress of humanity:

"Almost everything we call 'higher culture' is based on the spiritualization and intensification of cruelty" (106).

The Nazi glorification of hardness of character expressed itself in the utterly contemptuous and ruthless mistreatment of "racial inferiors" by SS men, the finest specimens of Aryan superiority... At the Nuremberg tribunal, the judges were horrified by the accused's total lack of "normal" human feelings, such as pity or regret, when crimes were mentioned... Indeed, the majority of SS officers

"had accepted a system of morality in which ordinary human feelings like conscience and compassion had no place. It was their duty to be hard: they boasted of their lack of feeling: they were beyond good and evil" (107).

It was as if the Nazis lived in another world, another order of things and of spirit, holding a totally different vision of the universe and a set of values transcending the conventional humanist concepts of "good" and "evil". Were they Martians? They were simply Nietzscheans, *"powerful, masterly, cruel and fearless"* (108), engaged in a sacred mission that should ultimately lead to the creation of the Superman, regardless of the human sacrifices it entailed...

Nietzsche in fact believed that *"the great majority of men have no right to existence, but are a misfortune to higher men"* (109), stressing on the need for a doctrine

"powerful enough to work as a breeding agent: strengthening the strong, paralyzing and destructive for the world-weary (110)... I teach: that there are higher and lower men, and that a single individual can under certain circumstances justify the existence of whole millennia- that is, a full, rich, great, whole human being in relation to countless incomplete fragmentary men" (111)... the real issue is the production of the synthetic man (112).

Quality matters, not quantity; nothing should stand in the way of the perfect man, the "whole man", even if it means the elimination of millions of worthless, wretched, uncreative, fragmentary lives: *"the magnitude of a 'progress' is gauged by the greatness of the sacrifice that it requires: humanity as a mass sacrificed to the prosperity of the one stronger species of man- that would be a progress"* (113)... Showing absolutely no consideration for the "miserable masses", Nietzsche combines the eugenicist idea of "breeding the most splendid types" with the idea of the selective extermination of human "failures": the Higher Men must *"gain that tremendous energy of greatness in order to shape the man of the future through breeding and, on the other hand, [through] the annihilation of millions of failures"* (114)... No statement could be more "Nazi" than the aforementioned one.

Nietzsche thus becomes the prophet of racial supremacy (that of the "Master Race" or the "aristocrats of blood and spirit") and the "preacher of death" for the slavish *Untermenschen*, as shown in this flagrant declaration:

"The earth is full of those to whom departure from life must be preached. The earth is full of the superfluous, life has been corrupted by the many-too-many (115)... the weak and the failures shall perish... And they shall be given every possible assistance" (116).

The Nazis only had to put Nietzsche's prophecy into practice: guided by an unshakable sense of mission, the SS, as "Sons of the gods", thought they had the legitimate right to enslave or kill any racial inferiors who stood in the way of the Superman: to Himmler,

"what happens to a Russian, to a Czech, does not interest me in the slightest (117) ... whether or not 10,000 Russian women collapse from exhaustion while digging a tank ditch interests me only in so far as the tank ditch is completed for Germany" (118).

Losses were never too high in Nazis' view, for *"the tragedy of greatness is to have to trample on corpses"* (119)... Indeed, life, for Nietzsche, was *"a scaffolding by means of which a select sort of being might rise to a higher sort of task and a higher sort of existence"* (120), a view shared by Nazism's equally (radically) aristocratic worldview which taught that *"the progress of humanity is like climbing an endless ladder; it is impossible to climb higher without first taking the lower steps"* (121).

CHAPTER FOUR

THE ARISTOCRATIC WORLDVIEW:

BREEDING THE ARYAN UNIVERSAL MASTER RACE

A. Socialism and Liberalism: the rule of the "Last Man"

"The Socialist's conception of the highest society is the lowest in the order of rank"

Friedrich Nietzsche

"The Jewish doctrine of Marxism rejects the aristocratic principle of nature and replaces the eternal privilege of power and strength by the mass of numbers and their dead weight"

Adolf Hitler

"Democracy represents the disbelief in great human beings and an elite society: 'everyone is equal to everyone else' "

Friedrich Nietzsche

"By rejecting the authority of the individual and replacing it by the numbers of some momentary mob, the parliamentary principle of majority rule sins against the basic aristocratic principle of nature"

Adolf Hitler

"Does this present not belong to the mob? mob above, mob below! What are 'poor' and 'rich' today! I unlearned this distinction!"

Friedrich Nietzsche

"The Western democracy of today is the forerunner of Marxism which without would not be thinkable. It provides this worldly plague with the culture in which its germs can spread"

Adolf Hitler

The right of the strong, higher men with "great souls", to dominate the weak, worthless and wretched "sub-humans", has clear political implications: it leads to a justification of highly authoritarian and elitist systems of government, such as the Third Reich... The rule of the Superman heralded by Nietzsche and Nazism will thus be a radically anti-democratic age, a repudiation of the humanist paradigm (both Liberal and Socialist) which has prevailed in the West since the Enlightenment and the French Revolution.

Indeed, while his proclamation of the "death of God" was a clear reaction to Christian Morality's transcendental and personal God, Nietzsche nonetheless believed that the Enlightenment's rationalism, with its narrow positivism and "realism", was definitely not the alternative for civilisation, for its rejection of the belief in the possibility of human greatness and perfection only leads to nihilism, and therefore could never create the Superman as mankind's highest goal, producing only "men without chests", i.e. modernity's contemptible race of mediocre uncreative "realists", men with horizontal virtue and limited souls:

"For thus you speak: 'We are complete realists, and without belief or superstition': thus you thump your chests- alas, even without having chests!…. Unworthy of belief: that is what I call you, you realists! … You are unfruitful: therefore you lack belief. But he who had to create always had his prophetic dreams and star-auguries- and he believed in belief!" (1).

We are reminded of Hitler's scorn of democracies for their lack of "true convictions", convictions that one defends with one's life, great ideals worth dying for.

The Nietzschean and Nazi philosophies were therefore a revolt against the entire humanist tradition of the West: Judaeo-Christianity, Rationalism, Socialism, and Liberalism, viewing the latter two as secularised versions of Christianity. Nietzsche and Nazism's avowed contempt for democracy and humanism led them to successfully establish a spiritual break with Western civilisation, a civilisation which they considered had fallen to the level of satisfying purely material, selfish and utilitarian 'values', thereby dismissing man's true vocation in life, which is none other than self-perfection and self-overcoming. Transcending nihilism thus required crushing these "enemies of the Superman" and their immediate cause, the French Revolution, what Nietzsche termed *"that gruesome … superfluous farce"* (2), with its *"wholly un-Germanic, genuinely neo-Latin, shallow, and unmetaphysical philosophy"* (3). According to Nietzsche, the French Revolution, the *"daughter and continuation of Christianity"*, corrupted humanity with its slogan "Liberty, Equality, Fraternity" for *all*, waging an all-out war *"against caste, against the noble, against the last privileges"* (4).

Rejecting both Socialism and Liberalism as two aspects of the same materialist and egalitarian view of the world, Nietzsche and Nazism condemned these "corrupt" theories for their levelling character which has led to a cult of the mediocre in all things by instituting the "lie of the equality of souls" as society's main foundation, as shown in Nietzsche's following declaration:

"Nobody today has the courage any longer for privileges, for masters' rights, for a sense of respect for oneself and one's peers- for a pathos of distance. Our politics is sick from this lack of courage. The aristocratic outlook was undermined from the deepest under-world through the lie of the equality of souls" (5).

Nietzsche thus dismisses both the "industrious democrats" and the "anarchist dogs", the "socialist dolts and blockheads" who all share a *"total and instinctive hostility to every form of society other than that of the autonomous herd (to the point of repudiating even the concepts 'master' and 'servant' -ni dieu ni maitre says a socialist formula-)"* being *"at one in their tenacious opposition to every special claim, every special right and privilege"* (6). Nietzsche's opposition to Socialism, which *"naively dreams of equal rights"*, and to parliamentary government and the press, *"the means by which the herd animal becomes master"* (7), is shared by Hitler, who views the Marxists' notion of a "classless society" as "sheer madness", while asserting that the democratic conception of a hierarchy based on money is no lesser madness, for they both replace the vital law and aristocratic principle of 'true domination' (which is racial and spiritual) by the numbers and their dead weight.

Liberalism and Socialism are therefore two sides of the same coin, and they only vary in degree, i.e. a socialist is a "super-democrat", a radical liberal of the left... While liberal democracy establishes an "un-natural" hierarchy (with a "fake elite" at the top) based on money, not true (moral, biological, spiritual) superiority, Socialism doesn't even recognize any hierarchy between men, and is thus a "remedy" worse than the (liberal) disease, an exacerbation of the materialistic, atomistic, individualistic, and utilitarian tendencies of Liberalism. Indeed, both ideologies focus on "capital" as the motor of history, clashing only on who should own and control it, the bourgeoisie or the proletariat... Addressing the rich bourgeois "upper classes", Nietzsche advises them first to cure themselves against their Capitalism as a prelude to cure the workman of his socialism:

"The only remedy against Socialism that still lies in your power is to avoid provoking socialism. Possession alone differentiates you from them" (8).

In a similar fashion, Hitler viewed the bourgeois world as "Marxist" but to a lesser degree, for it believed in the possibility of the domination of certain groups, whereas Marxism advocated a classless society:

"The Western democracy of today is the forerunner of Marxism which without it would not be thinkable. It provides this world plague with the culture in which its germs can spread" (9).

Against Socialism, *"the tyranny of the least and the dumbest"*, of the *"superficial and envious"*, a doctrine where there is badly hidden *"a will to negate life"* (10), Nietzsche directs the worst accusation, that of

"the collective degeneration… and diminution of man to the perfect herd animal… this animalisation of man to the pygmy animal of equal rights and equal pretensions" (11).

The "Socialist rabble" (whom Nietzsche despised the most) sought to impose the "injustice" of "equal rights to all" and thus infringe nature's aristocratic principle of the inequality of man: *"injustice never lies in unequal rights, it lies in the claim to 'equal' rights"* (12). The *"Socialist-Communist corruption"* (13), in Nietzsche's view, transformed the worker into a revengeful, envious anarchist who rejects all natural hierarchy; indeed, *"the socialists' conception of the highest society is the lowest in the order of rank"* (14).

The Nazis shared Nietzsche's utter contempt for Socialism; in fact, they were the staunchest enemies of Marxism, "that worldly plague". Thus, for Hitler, *"the Jewish doctrine"* of Marxism

"rejects the aristocratic principle of Nature and replaces the eternal privilege of power and strength by the mass of numbers and their dead weight. Thus it denies the value of personality in man, contests the significance of nationality and race, and thereby withdraws from humanity the premise of its existence and its culture" (15).

It is worth noting in this respect that National-Socialism was only "Socialist" in the sense of rejecting capitalism's "tyranny of money" (the same "hierarchy based on money" which Nietzsche condemned as "unnatural"), yet Nazism definitely condemned class conflict and the Socialist ideal of a "classless society", advocating instead a radically elitist and hierarchical system based on true superiority or 'true domination', i.e. the domination of race and personality, the rule of the best racial and spiritual elements of society, which would bring about the greatness of the whole nation, not the socialist atomistic "happiness of individuals"...

Second among the enemies of Nietzsche's "Superman" and Nazism's "New Order" are the Liberals, whom Nietzsche labelled the *"feebler descendants"* of *"Communists and Socialists of all times"* (16). Liberal democracy, which is *"Christianity made natural"* (17), also stands guilty -like Socialism- of instituting the "superstition" of the "equality of all before God"... To Nietzsche, Liberalism represents

"a common war on all that is rare, strange, privileged, the higher man, the higher soul, the higher duty, the higher responsibility, and the abundance of creative power" (18).

Therefore,

"the honorable term for mediocre is, of course, the word 'liberal' " (19).

In addition to their rejection of its egalitarian and levelling character, which only produces mediocrity, Nietzsche and Nazism also despise Liberalism's atomistic and ahistorical conception of the individual self and its realisation. Lacking any vision of the world and refusing to set as higher goal for humanity the possibility of perfection, the Liberal materialistic doctrine suffers from shallowness and superficiality, and therefore has never produced greatness or "made history", nor will it ever.

By declaring that *"Human society is an experiment... not a 'contract'!"* (20), Nietzsche launches a scathing attack against Liberalism's "contract theory", i.e. its conception of the state as a *"selfish State-less money-aristocracy"* (21), an attack which is echoed by Nazism's condemnation of

"that doctrine of licentiousness, of disconnectedness among individuals and -as a necessary result- of dictatorship by the will of the mass, composed of atomized individuals; a mass called into being, ...dominated and directed by money!" (22).

Liberalism thus represents the rule of money, while democracy represents the rule of the majority, and will lead, according to Nietzsche, to a *"levelling and mediocritising of man"* into a *"useful, industrious, highly serviceable and able herd-animal man... a type prepared for slavery in the subtlest sense"* (23)... This herd-animalisation, Nietzsche thought, is achieved through Parliamentary institutions, *"an adding-together of clever herd-men"* (24), an opinion shared by Hitler, who considers that *"by rejecting the authority of the individual and replacing it by the numbers of some momentary mob, the parliamentary principle of majority rule sins against the basic aristocratic principle of Nature" (25).*

Democracy is thus decadence assuming a political form... It represents, in Nietzsche's words, *"the disbelief in great human beings and an elite society: 'everyone is equal to everyone else' "*, whereas *"Aristocracy represents the belief in an elite humanity and higher caste"* (26).

In the light of the above-mentioned radically illiberal statements, one cannot but dismiss as utterly preposterous the allegations made by some scholars that Nietzsche was a Liberal humanist concerned with the sanctity and dignity of the ordinary individual. Nietzsche indeed distinguished between healthy, higher, or "heroic" egoism (i.e. the greatness of personality and individuality), and petty selfishness, the ahistorical, atomistic lower egoism of the Liberals. "Egoism", for the higher man, is the drive to increase the power of the soul; man's highest elevation is the attainment of his individuality, yet this process is limited to the select few born with noble souls, for whom happiness is self-overcoming, not mere comfort and self-preservation... Nietzsche's politics are in fact

"neither individualistic nor collectivistic. The former, he argues, 'does not recognise an order of rank and would grant one the same freedom as all', while the latter fails to generate a notion of individual greatness" (27).

Making sure his "heroic individualism" would not be confused with democratic individualism, Nietzsche sharply criticised the Liberal atomistic conception of freedom, which he condemned as being merely a "freedom from constraint" or "freedom from a yoke", asserting instead his own idea of freedom as victory or "higher freedom", the freedom of the warrior which grows out of overcoming, out of struggle, out of the Will to Power:

"Do you call yourself free? I want to hear your ruling idea, and not that you have escaped from a yoke.... Free from what? Zarathustra does not care about that! But your eye should clearly tell me: free for what?" (28).

According to Nietzsche and the Nazis, who belong to the noumenalist or teleo-naturalist school of thought, Liberal institutions are therefore *"injurers of freedom"* for *"they undermine the Will to Power"* (29), the freedom they advocate not being teleologically directed towards self-perfection. Scorning the liberal self-proclaimed, *"falsely named free spirits"* as an *"unfree and ludicrously superficial"* type of individuals, Nietzsche considered that they belonged *"among the levellers"* who strive after the

"universal green pasture happiness of the herd, with security, safety, comfort and an easier life for all….'equality' of rights' and 'sympathy for all that suffers' " (30).

Socialism, Liberalism, Democracy: for Nietzsche and the Nazis, these doctrines stand accused of having led humanity into modernity's "era of mediocrity", which represents the "victory of the slaves" (and their "petty virtues") or mob rule: *"does this present not belong to the mob?"* (31), deplores Nietzsche, adding:

"Mob above, mob below! what are 'poor' and 'rich' today! I unlearned this distinction" (32).

Indeed, despite differences in degree, not in nature, Socialism and Liberalism are inherently one and the same "decadent" materialistic and egalitarian paradigm, producing a levelling -and hence, a degeneration- of the nation into a herd society, which is, in Nietzsche's view, none other than

"a sum of zeroes- where every zero has 'equal rights', where it is virtuous to be zero" (33).

Nietzsche and Nazism had declared an all-out war against these avowed enemies of the Superman whose rule would be a spiritual, radically aristocratic age aimed at producing a collective elevation and self-overcoming of humankind towards greatness and perfection on earth, towards the creation of the God-Man.

Socialism and Liberalism thus represent the rule of "men without chests", the victory of the "Last Man", who is the *"beginning of the end"* (34), i.e. the herd-man of contemporary life which Nietzsche holds in contempt:

"Alas! The time is coming when man will give birth to no more stars. Alas! The time of the most contemptible man is coming… Behold! I shall show you the Ultimate Man. The earth has become small, and upon it hops the Ultimate Man, who makes everything small (35).

Ours is the age of the "Last Man", the antithesis to the Superman…

We are indeed living in the "Era of the Slave", a purposeless age of mediocrity in which greatness is absent and perfection, an impossibility... By imposing the Christian slogan of the "equality of souls before God", the French Revolution was responsible for producing the twin egalitarian and materialistic ideologies of Socialism and Liberalism, which are modern secularised versions of Christianity and which, far from achieving "progress", have reduced man into a "spiritual dwarf", a "perfect modern slave". Thus did Nietzsche and Nazism view modernity and the Judaeo-Christian Western civilisation... Christianity, with its notion of the transcendent and personal God, had ruled out the possibility of human perfection; only by "killing" this God would men be able to overcome themselves and become gods, for *"precisely this is Godliness, that there are gods but no God!"* (36)... One has to chose: either the greatness of the transcendent God or the greatness of the God-Man, the Inner God; one cannot have both, for one is always achieved at the expense of the other.

Yet, according to Nietzsche and Nazism, the materialistic Liberal and Socialist doctrines of the Enlightenment were certainly not the alternative to the transcendentalism of Christianity: indeed, although these doctrines had "killed God" for the sake of Man, their atheist materialism, by dismissing any possibility of self-overcoming and self-perfection, has turned man into a hedonistic pleasure-thirsty lustful creature, a slave to his desires and instincts, and has therefore led not only to a "dwarfing" of man, but also to an animalisation of man... to the "Last Man", the "lord and master" of the present:

"Overcome for me these masters of the present, O my brothers", urged Nietzsche, adding: "these petty people: they are the Superman's greatest danger!" (37).

The age of the Superman will be a radically aristocratic, anti-democratic age.

B. Aristocratic radicalism: Eugenics and the rule of the Aryan Master Race

The racist-aristocratic worldview: towards a New Aristocracy

"Aristocracy represents the belief in an elite humanity and higher caste"

"Justice speaks thus to me: 'men are not equal'. And they should not become

so, either!"

Friedrich Nietzsche

"We do not want to do away with inequalities between men, but, on the contrary, to increase them and make them into a principle protected by impenetrable barriers"

Adolf Hitler

"O my brothers, your nobility shall not gaze backward, but outward!... Let where you are going, not where you come from, henceforth be your honour!"

Friedrich Nietzsche

"The new aristocracy is being created on the basis of new law. Tradition is being replaced by ability. The Best One! This title is not inherited, it has to be earned!"

Heinrich Himmler

"For spirit alone does not make noble; rather, there should be something to ennoble the spirit- what is then required? Blood"

Friedrich Nietzsche

"True genius is always inborn and never cultivated, let alone learned... this applies not only to the individual man but also to the race"

Adolf Hitler

Arch enemies of the reign of ease and mediocrity so characteristic of modern times, the Nietzschean and Nazi doctrines destroyed all "old Law-tables" and condemned all "slave ideologies" (Judaeo-Christianity, Socialism, Liberalism, democracy...), advancing instead a radically elitist philosophy of life and view of the world: "Aristocratic radicalism" (38), a doctrine unique in the fact that it represents a 'third option' between 'corrupt egalitarian Democracy' and the 'materialist Socialism of the mob', while distinguishing itself from traditional aristocratic conservatism by its advocacy of a "new nobility" (of Platonic inspiration) based not on ownership of wealth or property, or an inherited title which one either does not deserve or does not live up to (as modern aristocracy has been reduced to), but rather on spiritual and biological (i.e. racial) superiority, merit, and achievement... all characteristics of a strong race, of the aristocrats of antiquity, the only true aristocrats... In other words, a nobility based on the Will to Power, on mental, moral, and physical superiority... Nietzsche indeed strove to re-establish, in a age of *suffrage universel,* the order of rank as an order of power (mental, moral, *and* physical power): *"what determines your rank is the quantum of power you are: the rest is cowardice"* (39). Justice is thus the will of the strongest (40).

Nietzsche believed that no true human excellence, greatness, creativity or nobility was possible except in aristocratic societies, whose members possessed -to a high degree- the "will to dominate" (41) arising out of *megalothymia,* i.e. the desire to be recognised as better than the others:

"Every elevation of the type 'man' has hitherto been the work of an aristocratic society- and so it will always be: a society which believes in a long scale of orders of rank and differences of worth between man and man" (42).

Aristocracy represents nature at its best, the supreme law of life and the only natural order, and thus, the ancient Indo-European "order of castes" of Brahmanism, based on the code of Manu -a radically elitist racial and spiritual system- should be re-established and serve as a model for the future:

"The order of castes, the supreme, the dominating law, is only the sanctioning of a natural order, a natural law of the first rank... Nature... separates from one another the predominantly spiritual type, the predominantly muscular and temperamental type, and the mediocre type- the last as the great majority, the first as the elite... the order of castes, order of rank, only formulates the supreme law of life itself" (43).

The Third Reich, a self-proclaimed modern Plato's Republic, was an attempt to set up the "order of castes" which Nietzsche praised as the highest model of an aristocratic system. The Nazis indeed believed -as Nietzsche did- that aristocracy represented the "rule of the best" (*aristos:* the best). The "ideal Reich" of the Nazis, in contrast to the "material Republic" of Socialists and Liberals, was a blueprint for Hitler's "New Order", a radically elitist system modelled on Nietzsche's much-celebrated Brahmanist caste system:

"What will the social order of the future be like? Comrades, I will tell you: there will be a class of overlords, and after them the rank and file of Party Members in hierarchical order, and then the great mass of anonymous followers, servants and worders in perpetuity, and beneath them, again all the conquered foreign races, the modern slaves. And over and above all

these there will reign a new and exalted nobility" (44).

In other words, a racial-spiritual hierarchy quite similar to the Indo-Aryan "order of castes".

Men are radically unequal: therefore, the strongest and most gifted individuals in spirit and intellect should rule the majority of weak and worthless *Untermenschen*. Any attempt to impose equality is thus considered immoral, for justice itself is inequality; thus spoke Nietzsche:

" *'Equality for equals, inequality for unequals' - that would be the true voice of justice: and, what follows from it, 'Never make equal what is unequal' (45)... Justice speaks thus to me: 'Men are not equal.' And they should not become so, either!" (46).*

Adopting Nietzsche's admittedly illiberal and inegalitarian politics of domination, Hitler declares:

"We do not want to do away with inequalities between men, but, on the contrary, to increase them and make them into a principle protected by impenetrable barriers" (47).

The Nazis opposed to the Liberal state of *"equality of all citizens with equal rights, equal duties,"* the National Socialist state of *"inequality of all folk comrades, with unequal duties, unequal rights,"* thus creating *"a new society with new disparities, new relationships"* (48), for only spiritual elitism (Aristocracy) can lead to human greatness, while materialist egalitarianism (Democracy, Liberalism, Socialism, ...) only leads to mediocrity...

A characteristic feature of Nietzsche's "Aristocratic radicalism" -which the Nazis wholly espoused- is the call for the creation of a "new nobility", a community of godlike Supermen who would replace the outdated traditional aristocracy, based on ascription, as well as the modern "money-aristocracy" (as Nietzsche calls it), based on wealth, the latter despised by both Nietzsche and Hitler (the Fuehrer indeed stressed on the fact that *"talent is not bound up with the higher walks of life, let alone with wealth"* [49]). Only a new aristocracy would bring back greatness to this world in decay: *"Therefore, O my brothers"*, wrote Nietzsche,

"is a new nobility needed: to oppose all mob-rule and all despotism and to write anew upon new law-tables the word: 'Noble'. For many noblemen are needed, and noblemen of many kinds, for nobility to exist! Or, as I once said in a parable: 'Precisely this is godliness, that there are gods but

no God!' " (50).

The SS claimed they were that "new nobility" of blood and spirit of Nietzsche's prophecy, and their leadership encouraged its members, from the beginning, to develop a *Herrenbewusstsein* (master consciousness) as individuals and an *Elitebewusstsein* (elite consciousness) as a group (51).

Why a "new" nobility? What's wrong with the "old" one (the traditional aristocracy), or the "actual" one (the financial "elite")? Staunch opponents of all materialism, Nietzsche and the Nazis believed that true superiority is never based on wealth, for the latter is merely something we *have*, not something we *are*. Therefore, today's "money-aristocracy" is a fake elite, only distinguished from the poor "lower classes" by virtue of its possession, not by virtue of its inherent spiritual or moral worth, as was the case in antiquity, where social hierarchy was based on true superiority... As regards the traditional aristocracy, Nietzsche, totally in line with his aristocratic radicalism (and despite the fact that he is sometimes classified as a "neo-aristocratic conservative"), criticised the conservatives, arguing that, granted that tradition was to be revered and respected, it was nonetheless neither possible nor desirable to recapture the virtues of the past which, on their own, would not be able to bring the aristocrats back to power:

"O my brothers, your nobility shall not gaze backward, but outward!... Let where you are going, not where you come from, henceforth be your honour!" (52).

The aristocracy and monarchy of the past are thus to be replaced by the new "Lords of the earth", who are even higher than kings:

"The age of kings is past: what today calls itself the people deserves no king... What do kings matter any longer!...We are on our way to find the Higher Man- the man who is higher than we: although we are kings, for the highest man should also be the highest lord on earth" (53).

The Third Reich's "new aristocracy", the SS, was similarly opposed to a return to the past; it was *"being created on the basis of new law. Tradition is being replaced by ability. The Best One! This title is not inherited, it has to be earned"* (54). Racial (i.e. biological *and* moral) superiority, as well as merit and achievement, henceforth determined social status. The Nazis had

"new standards, a new way of appraising. The little word 'von' no longer means to us the same thing it once did. We believe that a nobility has the

right to exist, not a nobility of class, not a nobility of birth or of property,
but a nobility of achievement (Leistung)... the best from all classes, ...
that is the nobility of the Third Reich" (55).

In the words of Heinrich Himmler, the Reichsfuehrer SS,

"we want to create an upper class for Germany, selected constantly over
centuries, a new aristocracy, recruited always from the best sons and
daughters of our nation, an aristocracy that never becomes old" (56).

In their call for the rule of superior men who were to be continuously
chosen from all classes, both Nietzsche and the Nazis were highly inspired
by Plato's aristocratic class of "Guardians", whose members were to be
recruited from all walks of life, for true superiority is spiritual, therefore
inborn, and not material, that is, related to acquired titles or possessions,
i.e. to socio-economic status. The "little word 'von' " to which the Nazis
gave a whole new meaning, also meant much more than a mere inherited
title to Nietzsche, who was keen to specify that when he defended the
"nobility of birth and blood", he was *not speaking here of the little word*
'von' or of the Almanach de Gotha" (57)... The new nobility would be a
nobility of blood and spirit, a nobility based on race, and, because the
Aryan race was clearly superior to others, its elite members were deemed
natural aristocrats and thus belonged to the universal Master Race.

The "aristocratic radicalism" advocated by Nietzsche and the Nazis
was thus clearly not an apology for the rule of the wealthiest or those who
wield the most military power; in contrast to the "financial elite" and the
"political elite" of today, the Nietzschean and Nazi "New Nobility" of the
future would be a "natural elite" of "born Masters", a nobility based on
"blood" (i.e. race *and* class, which are identical to Nietzsche, who spoke
of a "social race" and a "master race") as well as "spirit"; i.e. a "synthetic
nobility" combining biological *and* spiritual superiority. Indeed, although
Nietzsche did assert that the noble caste's superiority lay *not in their*
physical strength, but primarily in their psychical- they were more complete
human beings" (58), stressing on *"the belief in a nobility by birth in moral*
matters, too" (59), he was even more emphatic that "blood", or the innate
superiority of the aristocrat (and not just his transmitted social privilege,
represented by the title "von"), which has nothing to do with education
or the environment, was an equally essential attribute of superiority as
"spirit":

"There is only nobility of birth, only nobility of blood [I am not speaking

here of the little word 'von' or of the Almanach de Gotha: parenthesis for asses]. When one speaks of 'aristocrats of the spirit,' reasons are usually not lacking for concealing something; as is well known, it is a favourite term among ambitious Jews. For spirit alone does not make noble; rather, there must be something to ennoble the spirit. - What then is required? Blood" (60).

There can be no clearer statement of Nietzsche's belief that the order of rank is essentially a matter of inheritance, a matter of birth, a matter of genes, and not simply a matter of "talent" or acquired ability, as Bluhm and Kaufmann have argued... The above-mentioned statement indeed sharply contradicts Bluhm and Kaufmann's assertions that when Nietzsche speaks of "aristocrats", he is *only* referring to the "aristocrats of spirit" (*"a favourite term among ambitious Jews"*), not to the aristocrats of blood. It is worth noting, in this respect, the curious insistence of both Kaufmann and Bluhm on reducing Nietzsche's conception of aristocracy to a mere "intellectual elite" of acquired superiority, instead of the innate biological-spiritual superiority so characteristic of the Nietzschean "synthetic" nobility, a nobility of "complete individuals" or "whole men" representing both biological *and* spiritual superiority, i.e. the *"union of spiritual superiority with well-being and an excess of strength"* (61). One indeed feels compelled to ask whether behind Bluhm and Kaufmann's insistence to label Nietzsche's new nobility "aristocrats of the spirit" with no reference whatsoever to "blood", *"reasons are usually not lacking for concealing something"* ...

Nietzsche therefore believes that true genius is innate, never acquired:

"Against the doctrine of the influence of the milieu and external causes: the force within is infinitely superior; much that looks like external influence is merely its adaptation from within... A genius is not explained in terms of such conditions of his origin" (62).

One is *born* superior; one does not *become* superior. The Nazis, too, sought to create this "synthetic aristocracy" (the SS) endowed with both biological *and* spiritual superiority, i.e. a "racial aristocracy", a Nietzschean "nobility of blood" and *not* of social rank (or rather a nobility of social rank *determined by* blood):

"In place of a traditional social elite, Heinrich Himmler envisioned a racial elite based on the purity of blood, equating superior racial traits

with manifest ability as well as character. Old elites based on transmitted social privileges were to be replaced by a new synthetic aristocracy, created in the mould of a community organized and determined along racial lines... Attempts to put into practice the vision of an elite of blood were mirrored in the fervent exertion expended in the biological screening of potential SS candidates" (63).

In the "new aristocracy", it is your "blood" (i.e. your psycho-biological make-up) which determines your social rank; it is therefore a hierarchy based on true, *innate* superiority (which is spiritual *and* biological), and not fake superiority based on *acquired* privileges such as inherited titles or property.

The order of rank, or hierarchy, is the order of life, the natural order... Men are not equal nor shall they become equal: this is a supreme truth sanctioned by nature itself. The whole world being hierarchically structured, inequality applies to all living creatures, to individuals as well as to entire races: that it how Nietzsche and the Nazis viewed the world; their "aristocratic radicalism" applied to the entire universe; it was a "racist-aristocratic worldview" (*Rassenaristokratischer Weltanschauung*), linking race with class, or racial superiority with social superiority. Indeed, racism and elitism are closely intertwined: elitism is a form of racism, and racism is inherently elitist... Both Nietzsche and the Nazis thus recognised the existence of elite races (the "Master Race") and elites *within* races (the "Higher Men"):

Let us admit to ourselves unflinchingly how every higher culture has hitherto begun! Men of a still natural nature, barbarians in every fearful sense of the word, men of prey still in possession of an unbroken strength of will and lust for power, threw themselves upon weaker, more civilised, more peaceful, perhaps trading or cattle-raising races, or upon old mellow cultures, the last vital forces in which were even then flickering out in a glittering firework display of spirit and corruption" (64)...

Nietzsche's endorsement of the superiority of some races to others *"lends support to a general principle of ethnic or racial discrimination"*... In his unpublished notes, he sometimes suggests *"that entire races (judged decadent) ought to be exterminated and/or bred out of existence"* (65). Nietzsche viewed an individual's true superiority in terms of biology and physiology (in addition to spirit, naturally) rather than in social and political terms. He did admit the existence of *"great inequalities of biological capacity"* (66), asserting that the difference between men is so great that it compels us to speak of "two distinct species". Significantly, it was Darwin who declared in the *Descent of Man* that *"the varieties of mankind are so distinct that similar differences found in any other animal would warrant their classification in different species, if not in different genera"* (67). The Nazis, as neo-Social Darwinists, asserted the existence of a natural hierarchy among races as well as *within* races. By proclaiming that *"true genius is always inborn and never cultivated, let alone learned... this applies not only to the individual man but also to the race"* (68), Hitler was justifying the leadership by an elite within racial groups in what came to be known as the *Fuehrersprinzip* or "leadership principle".

The Aryan race: a Master Race of blood and spirit

"The conquering and master race- the Aryan race... The best endowed and most reflective species of man"

Friedrich Nietzsche

"Scarcely any one will have the hardihood to deny that the inhabitants of Northern Europe have become the makers of the world's history"

Houston Stewart Chamberlain

"Human culture and civilisation... are inseparably bound up with the presence of the Aryan... You find in him the magnificent alliance of the most splendid physical beauty with the shining spirit and the nobility of the soul"

Adolf Hitler

According to Nietzsche, the best class, the best race, should prevail; mankind should set as its highest goal the breeding of the coming elite, of the "new aristocracy" of the future, a higher, stronger species of man, a Master Race most highly gifted in intellect and will, destined to rule the earth:

"It is a comfort to me to know that above the steam and filth of human lowlands there is a higher, brighter humanity, very small in number (for everything outstanding is by its nature rare)" (69).

In Nietzsche's view, these "Higher Men" should become the "Lords of the earth" and the "lawgivers of the future", for they are the forerunners of the Superman. "Lords of the earth" is a familiar expression in *Mein*

Kampf... It is indeed beyond doubt that Hitler perceived the Aryans as the Supermen, the "Master Race" of Nietzsche's prophecy; the Aryan, or Nordic, was that superior man in spirit and biology, in beauty and intellect, in moral and physical perfection. It is as though Nazism was a will to create this Nietzschean Superman through biological and moral experiments, resulting in the ultimate verdict: the Aryan is a Superman in the making, the ideal man worshipped by Nietzsche. We feel as though Nietzsche was calling for the formation of an institution such as the SS racial elite, as an actualisation of his preaching:

"You solitaries of today, you who have seceded from society, you shall one day be a people: from you, who have chosen out yourselves, shall a chosen people spring- and from this chosen people, the Superman" (70).

The SS had answered Nietzsche's call, a call they were convinced was addressed to them, for they claimed to be the Master Race (significantly, *the* central theme in both the Nietzschean and Nazi doctrines), i.e. the best class of the best race, the "racial aristocracy" who had the legitimate right to rule over 'lower humanity'.

What is unique about Nietzsche's "Master Race", or *Herrenvolk*- a term which was to become a favourite Nazi war-cry- is the fact that it is at the same time a race *and* a class: it includes the aristocrats of blood *and* spirit, a higher race of men forming the aristocracy of humanity... Indeed, Nietzsche often uses the terms "race" and "class" interchangeably, for he considers them as one and the same, defining class as *"a social race"* (71), and affirming that *"genealogical and racial differences are also brought out in the classes"* (72); one should not underestimate the biological component in class, the biological capacities which vary between classes (*"for spirit alone does not make noble, rather...blood!"*). This "biological" or "racial" determinism has considerable implications, namely: that a higher class is also a higher race, that mankind's culture-creating, strong races are also mankinds' aristocracy. Significantly, that was precisely the same correlation between race and class that the Nazis made when they declared that the Aryans were the *Herrenvolk*, the aristocracy of humanity...

It is indeed undeniable that Nietzsche's coming "Master Race" is a real distinctive race, a "stronger species" of Supermen. The "problem of race", according to Nietzsche, lies in the fact that

"it is simply not possible that a human being should not have the qualities or preferences of his parents and ancestors in his body, whatever appearances

may suggest to the contrary... A 'plebeian nature' is fixed once acquired, and always passed on as 'corrupted blood' " (73).

The "strong" and the "weak" are therefore two distinct "races" -even species- of man, and consequently, two different classes.

Yet who is this "higher aristocracy", this "higher race" of Supermen whose breeding Nietzsche and the Nazis considered as mankind's highest goal? To the Nazis, it was undeniably the Aryans, i.e. the Nordics (in the racial, not geographic sense), also known as the Germanic or Teutonic race - although the latter two terms are cultural, not racial, and hence have been wrongfully used to describe the Aryan race, which is trans-national, not limited to geography or culture. It is useful in this context, and before going further, to briefly mention the Nazi theory concerning the Aryan race, according to which the Nordics are the purest racial representatives of the original Aryan race. Indeed, according to most ethnologists, Scandinavia was the birthplace of the Aryan race, and hence, *"the first Aryans were Nordics"* (74). There are several theories regarding the origin of the Aryan race: whereas most Aryanist occultists (especially Karl Haushofer, the spiritual guide of the Nazi movement) believed that the Aryan race originated in Central Asia, most ethnologists argue that the Aryans came from Northern Europe. Nevertheless, all agree on the biological and spiritual characteristics and superiority of the Aryan race.

According to Nazi racial theory, the Aryan racial type, i.e. the Nordic type, represents the pure white race, the other two main branches of the "white" race- the Alpine (i.e. the Celts and Slavs) and Mediterranean races, being mixtures of the Aryan race with non-white "inferior races" such as the Mongols (producing the Alpine race and its East-Baltic, or Slavic, sub-race), and the Semites and Alpines (producing the Mediterranean race). It is worth noting in this respect that the term "Nordic" should be understood as a purely racial, and not a geographic, term, and is therefore not restricted to Northern Europe; indeed, many Finns, Swedes, Danes are not *racially* Nordic, rather Alpine! Conversely, Nordics —in the racial sense (i.e. Aryans)- can be found all over Europe (including in Mediterranean countries) and —albeit to a lesser degree- in some parts of Asia; and many Nordics in non-Nordic nations are more pure than some Germans or Norwegians... The term "Nordic", for ethnologists, is in fact the racial term for "Aryan" (and thus they are used interchangeably in this book, together with "Germanic"), and it was used to describe Aryans simply because most of the representatives of this race are found in Northern Europe; the same goes for the "Mediterranean" and "Alpine" races, which are also used as purely racial, not geographic terms, among ethnologists. Nevertheless, Nazi racial theory advocates that Nordics could also be found all over the globe due to the Nordic migrations and invasions of Europe, Asia, America, etc (the same applies to the Alpine and Mediterranean races, which can also be found anywhere on earth due to racial mixture).

Thus, according to the Nazi doctrine, the Aryans, who invaded Northern India (hence the name "Indo-European", "Indo-Aryan", or "Indo-Germanic"), the whole of Europe, Scandinavia, Asia Minor, the Levant, Persia, Tibet, ... were the only culture-founding race, the only creative force in human history. Specifically, Hitler argued that the civilisations of India, Persia, Egypt, Greece, and Rome were Aryan creations, the product of Nordic immigrants or invasions. Similarly, the French ethnologist and philosopher Arthur de Gobineau identified the "true Aryans" with the "Aryas" ("Noblemen"; the Sanskrit word *Arya* meaning "Nobility"), the dominant caste of India (of pure Nordic stock), as well as *the Persians, the Hellenes, and the Sarmates or ancestral Germans* (75), while H.S. Chamberlain saw history and civilisation as the product of *Der Germane* ("the Teuton": the Aryan):

"Scarcely any one will have the hardihood to deny that the inhabitants of Northern Europe have become the makers of the world's history" (76).

Based on these historical and ethnological facts, Hitler proudly announced the ultimate verdict:

"Human culture and civilisation... are inseparably bound up with the presence of the Aryan" (77).

Civilisation and Aryanism were indissolubly considered as one and the same... By his great achievements in culture and civilisation throughout history, the Aryan has proven that he has a superior spirit; therefore, the Aryanists concluded, his superiority must be related to his genes, to his biological as well as mental make-up.

In the Nazis' view, the Aryans, or Nordics, formed the aristocracy of humanity; they were the Master Race of Nietzsche's vision, for they were the legendary "Aryas", or noblemen, of history, a higher race as well as a higher caste. Greatly influenced by the anthropo-sociological school founded by the French anthropologist G. Vacher de Lapouge and the German Otto Ammon, the Nazis adopted *the law of social stratification, or the asserted superiority of the tall, dolichocephalic* [long head, oval, narrow face] *blond, the genuine Teutonic or Nordic type*", who was *"particularly frequent among the upper classes"* (78) in most nations, while the short and stocky brachycephalic (short head, round, broad face) brunet, the Alpine type, was predominant among the lower classes. In other words, the upper classes are predominantly Aryan, whereas the lower classes are mainly Alpine or Mediterranean... Of course, according to this theory, this classification hardly applies to today's Western societies, which are mainly ruled by wealth, not talent or racial superiority, as in ancient aristocratic epochs; nevertheless, it still relatively and partly applies to a number of non-Western countries such as Iran, India, etc, where some members of the upper classes are still predominantly Aryan, despite the racial inter-mixture between castes and classes.

Equating race with class, in Nietzsche's fashion, the Nazis embraced the doctrine of the "social selectionists" or anthropo-sociologists (Lapouge, Ammon, Collignon, ...) who readily discerned in the struggle of classes in modern industrial centres, *"a new form of the age-old struggle of races"* (79), a struggle mainly opposing the dolichocephalic aristocrats and the brachycephalic herdmen. Indeed, according to the anthropo-sociologists and the Nazis, the shape of the human skull (the general proportions of the length, breadth, and height, i.e. the cephalic index) is the most characteristic mark of difference between races, a *"decidedly more permanent racial characteristic than pigmentation"* (80), for it *"determined psychic qualities"* (81): *"it is the quality and not the quantity of the brain that is the cause of intellectual capacity"* (82), i.e. it is the head form which determines the brain's capacity. The Nazis were first and foremost craniologists, and SS candidates had to undergo a crucial racial examination whereby their skulls −along with their whole morphology− were measured in order to determine whether they were pure −or at least predominantly- Aryans. Race, therefore, is −or should be- the only true criterion of social status and mental superiority: the Nordic's intellectual and spiritual superiority is hence explained by his unique and perfect head form (slightly dolichocephalic- cephalic index of around 75 − i.e. perfect proportions between the head width, length, and height), the 'golden mean' between the extreme dolichocephaly of the Semite and the Negro, and the brachycephaly of the Alpine (Celt, Slav), the Mongol, and most of today's Mediterraneans (who, as already mentioned, are mixtures between Semites, Alpines, and the original, predominantly Aryan dolichocephalic Mediterraneans). It is most significant, in this respect, to mention Nietzsche's clearly racist condemnation of the "physiological deterioration" of the *"conquering and master race- the Aryan race"* due to racial mixture, brought about by the reign of democracy and socialism and the predominance of the round-headed Alpine

"dark-haired, pre-Aryan subject race... which has obtained the upper hand in the whole of Europe in complexion and the shortness of the skull, and perhaps in the intellectual and social qualities" (83)...

This statement is of particular importance, for not only does it reveal Nietzsche's Aryan racism, but it also shows that Nietzsche -exactly like the anthropo-sociologists and later the Nazis- linked the head form with mental capacity and social status, thus adopting the Nordic doctrine of the superiority of the Aryan race.

Nietzsche in fact extensively employs racial -or rather racist- Aryanist terminology (a fact which scholars like Hollingdale, Kaufmann or Bluhm simply chose to ignore...), making frequent references to Aryans as the "conquering and Master Race"... and praising the "magnificent blonde Teuton beast"... For Nietzsche, indeed, it was the ancient Northern peoples of Europe who possessed the physical and moral superiority so characteristic of an aristocratic race, especially the ancient Germans (not today's racially-mixed, liberal Germans!), who displayed *"a number of virtues more manly than any that other European countries can show"* (84)... a statement which led a scholar to comment: *"to anyone who knows the supreme value Nietzsche set on what he called 'manly', the above passage is final. The Nazis have had no trouble in adopting him as their prophet"* (85). Many other statements by Nietzsche are overtly Aryanist, revealing his Aryan racism, such as his praise of Manu, *"the racially purest Aryan law-book"* (86), *"an incomparably spiritual and superior work"* which he held in the highest esteem, for it was *"the product of the ruling class"* (87) representing pure Aryan humanity, with *"noble values everywhere, a feeling of perfection, an affirmation of life"* (88), as opposed to Christianity, *"the reaction against that morality of breeding, of race, of privilege... the Anti-Aryan religion par excellence... the revaluation of all Aryan values"* (89), a religion which thus first needed to be "barbarised, Germanised" in order to be accepted by the war-like manly Teutons (90).

Calling for a revival of "the Aryan order of castes" (91) characterised by the rule of the noble Indo-European "Aryas" (92) over the subjugated dark-skinned aborigines of India, Nietzsche on more than one occasion specifically describes the Aryan race as the Master Race (only once including the non-Aryan Japanese and Arabic nobility among the aristocratic races, yet along with the Roman and German nobility, the Homeric heroes, and the Scandinavian Vikings (93), all of Aryan stock…). When Nietzsche says: *"it is quite in order that we possess no religion of oppressed Aryan races, for that is a contradiction: a Master race is either on top or it is destroyed"* (94), or when he says of the Aryan race that it is *"the best endowed and most reflective species of man"* (95), the *"conquering and master race"* (96), Nietzsche leaves no room for controversy over the Aryan identity of his "Master Race". Similarly, by praising the *"splendid blond beast"*, he is not only referring to the blondness of the lion (an allusion to the aristocratic races), but also using the term "blond beast" as a racial concept (97), an allusion to the characteristic blondness of the Nordic peoples; indeed, Nietzsche is crystal-clear when he specifically calls the "noble Teutons" *"the fairest specimens of the 'blond beast' "* (98), or when he admires *"the wrath of the blonde Teuton beast"* (99) who terrorised the "weaker" non-Aryan races of Europe… The "magnificent blond beast" thus refers to the fair-haired "Aryan Master Race" that dominated European antiquity, the noble Aryas or ancient Aryans, in contrast to the darker hair of the (pre-Aryan) peoples they subjugated:

"The vulgar man can be distinguished as the dark-coloured, and above all as the black-haired ("hic niger est"), as the pre-Aryan inhabitants of the Italian soil, whose complexion formed the clearest feature of distinction from the dominant blondes, namely the Aryan conquering race" (100).

Elsewhere, Nietzsche takes "for granted" that the Negroes are *"representative of the prehistoric man"* (101), i.e. primitive creatures later described by Hitler as *"monstrosities halfway between man and ape"*… Based on such statements, how can one ignore, or even deny- as Kaufmann and Bluhm do- that Nietzsche did have racist views, that he did affirm the superiority of the Aryan, that he did despise the "pre-Aryan" primitive races, deploring the "physiological deterioration" of the "Aryan conquering and Master Race" through racial inter-mixture?

All of the above-mentioned facts and evidence thus lead to the following certainty: that Nietzsche's much-celebrated "Master Race" is undoubtedly the Aryan race, whose uncontested superiority was proclaimed by the Nazis… Could Nietzsche be more "Nazi" in this respect? When Hitler praised the *"magnificent alliance of the most splendid physical beauty with the shining spirit and the nobility of the soul"* so characteristic of the Aryan, he was in fact describing the Superman of Nietzsche and his highly-praised "splendid blond Teuton beast" and "Aryan Master Race" that represents human perfection, holding the monopoly of beauty, intelligence, and strength. The characteristics of Nietzsche's "race" of Supermen have indeed striking similarities with the physical, intellectual, and moral qualities of the Aryan race venerated by Hitler, Rosenberg, Gobineau and Chamberlain: as regards physical appearance, the Nazis had no trouble assimilating Nietzsche's "strong and beautiful race" of "blond Teuton beasts" with the splendid rosy-skinned, light-haired and bright-eyed Nordic race, which they described as aesthetically and biologically perfect, the most beautiful, strongest, and healthiest race on earth, having perfect proportions, or measurements, according to Nazi racial criteria: high stature, broad shoulders, a slim and well-proportioned body, long legs, and especially -for that is the most important characteristic of racial, mental, and spiritual superiority- a cephalic index of around 75 (i.e. slightly long-headed, or dolichocephalic), a facial index above 90, and a prominent occiput, as well as a narrow oval face whose smooth parts (particularly the narrow forehead, narrow lower jaw, and prominent chin) support the expression of clean-cut, well-defined physiognomy: in other words, the Aryan is the ideal of beauty on earth, the perfect representation of a Greek god, as Hans Guenther, the main theorist of the Nordic race, affirmed:

"If an illustrator, painter, or sculptor wants to represent the image of a bold, goal-determined, resolute person, or of a noble, superior, and heroic human being, he will in most cases create an image which more or less approximates the image of the Nordic race. He will also create a man who will be regarded as a typical representation of the upper social strata." (102).

So much for aesthetics... Biology, for both Nietzsche and the Nazis, is only the form, not the content; "blood" is essential, for it is a pre-condition for greatness, but it is not greatness-in-itself. A strong and healthy body should thus be accompanied by a "great soul", for spirit takes precedence over the body; therefore, the real criterion of superiority is the moral, spiritual one; and here is where the similarities between the Aryan and the Superman of Nietzsche are the most striking; the following characteristic spiritual and moral qualities of the Germanic race- as described by Gobineau, Chamberlain, Guenther, Rosenberg, ... are indeed those of a Master Race worthy of Nietzsche's highest praise: individuality; uniqueness; a great soul; overflowing energy; boldness, courage; a heroic disposition; nobility; pride; a strong sense of honour, loyalty, duty, and sacrifice; an inclination to knightly justice; a higher intelligence; a feeling of superiority; aggressiveness; a free and independent spirit; creativity; ambition; sincerity; a longing for self-overcoming; discipline; idealism, mysticism, but also a definite faculty of judgement, a sense of reality and rejection of miracles; a spirit of exploration and invention; and, most important- a strong will power... In short, the values and virtues of the Superman, the characteristics of an aristocratic class, which is in a sense a distinct "race", for race is both biological and moral... Indeed, both Nietzsche and the Nazis had a psycho-biological conception of "race", repudiating the strict division between the body and the spirit. Nietzsche had in fact utter contempt for Christianity's teaching that a "perfect soul" could be

"carried about in a cadaver of a body, and to do so needed to concoct a new conception of 'perfection': a pale, sickly, idiot-fanatic condition- so-called 'holiness' ", holiness itself being "a symptom-syndrome of the impoverished, enervated, incurably corrupted body!" (103)

We are reminded of Hitler's condemnation of Liberal Democracy's attempt to create men out of *"monstrosities halfway between man and ape"* (104)... The Nazis believed in a "biological mystic" or a "mystical biology", espousing the neo-pagan ideology called "metagenetics", i.e. the idea *"that the 'biological' and the 'spiritual' heritage of a person or people are ontologically identical"* (105); in other words, a higher soul always dwells in a higher body. In determining the superiority of the Nordic race, therefore, Guenther -the racist philosopher- believes that *"physical appearance is involved, for the body is the showplace of the soul"* - he indeed uses anthropological measurements of skulls, etc, as well as descriptions of a race's outward appearance, as criteria of racial superiority- But, to him, *"the soul is primary"*... (106).

Nietzsche is even more emphatic in establishing the importance of the body, glorifying "blood" as the essential counterpart of the spirit, the means of breeding the Superman, the synthetic man:

"Belief in the body is more fundamental than belief in the soul: the latter arose from unscientific reflection on [the agonies of] the body" (107)... Belief in the body is always a stronger belief than belief in the spirit; and whoever desires to undermine it, also undermines at the same time most thoroughly belief in the authority of the spirit!... (108)... perhaps the entire evolution of the spirit is a question of the body; it is the history of the development of a higher body that emerges into our sensibility... In the long run, it is not a question of man at all: he is to be overcome" (109).

In Nietzsche's eyes, culture draws upon heredity, yet takes the spirit no less than the body; greatness is thus always a function of the "whole man", the creative genius with a higher body and spirit. Though glorifying blood, Nietzsche nonetheless does not renounce spirit, "the force within" which is "infinitely superior" than the influence of the milieu and external causes:

> *"Much that looks like external influence is merely its adaptation from within... A genius is not explained in terms of such conditions of his origin" (110)... Spirit is "the essential thing in the life process... the tremendous shaping, form-creating force working from within which utilises and exploits 'external circumstances' " (111).*

The Nazis, too, did not *only* glorify blood, as is widely believed: it is true that exoterically, Nazism seemed like "nothing more than applied biology" (112); yet esoterically, the Nazi conception of "race" transcended *mere* genetics and biological determinism, or rather, it was a mystic-biological, meta-genetic notion. Race was linked to biology as well as *Geist* ("spirit"), the latter taking precedence over the former. Although the spiritual make-up of the person was intimately and closely related to his biological make-up, *"the soul"* was *"primary"*. The fact which means that the characteristic moral qualities of the Aryans *could* -exceptionally- also be found among non-Aryan individuals, as a result of the racial inter-mixture of the Nordic race with "lower races": as Gobineau explains, although the white race (the Aryans he considered the original white race, and hence "the jewel of the white race")

> *"originally possessed the monopoly of beauty, intelligence and strength, by its union with other varieties hybrids were created, which were beautiful without strength, strong without intelligence, or, if intelligent, both weak and ugly" (113).*

Therefore, not all "biological" Aryans are Aryans in the moral sense; conversely, some individuals who are not biologically "pure Aryans" nonetheless could exhibit a typical "Aryan spirit" and thus be considered as "true Aryans" (provided that they possess a substantial amount of Aryan blood, for the biological make-up is necessary). This applied to some of the highest-ranking Nazi officials such as Goebbels, Himmler and Goering... The Third Reich's philosopher, Alfred Rosenberg, confirms this mystic-biological notion of "race" by saying that, although the Nordic race exhibits particular biological and moral traits, yet *"the inner soul and outward physical traits do not always correspond"*; therefore, *"it would be superficial to judge individuals by their cephalic indices; conduct and achievement are a better criterion"* (114). Race is not only physical in nature; thus, the "biological determinism" of the Nazis is not absolute...

The fact which makes them true Nietzscheans... H.S. Chamberlain, whose racial views were wholly adopted by the Nazis, asserts that a Nordic soul could inhabit a non-Nordic body: *"Germanism does not lie in the blood, but in the mind* (115)... *Whoever reveals himself German by his acts, whatever be his genealogical tree, is a German"* (116). Chamberlain advocated "mental, spiritual and intellectual Aryanism" transcending mere biological Aryanism, and thus anticipating the "spiritual racism" which the Nazis later preached, *"another kind of racialism, deeper and no doubt more horrible..."* (117), for it believed that the inequality among races was not only a biological inequality, but also -and even more so- a metaphysical, spiritual inequality: just as there were "higher races" and "lower races", there were also "higher souls" and "lower souls"... This explains Hitler's description of the Jew as a "degenerate" species, a "non-being" who is "even lower than the animal", being "as remote from the animal as the animal is from man"... The Jew, in Hitler's view, is "alien to the natural order"; he is not only biologically inferior, but also -and even more so- mentally and spiritually inferior ... This also accounts for Nietzsche's contempt for the Jew, the "supreme decadent" and the "typical slave", as we shall see in the chapter on anti-Semitism.

Eugenics: the conscious and organised breeding of the Master Race

"Not 'mankind' but Overman is the goal!... Our way is upward, from the species across to the super-species"

Friedrich Nietzsche

"Aryan man is the highest image of the Lord, the only true species of man, the species with potential for evolution"

Adolf Hitler

"The coming Master Race would arise as a result of a fundamental, artificial and conscious breeding of... a higher type of dominating and Caesarian spirits... the real issue is the production of the synthetic man"

"You solitaries of today, you who have seceded from society; you shall one day be a people; from you, who have chosen out yourselves, shall a chosen people spring- and from this chosen people, the Superman"

Friedrich Nietzsche

"The Fuehrer's task was a greater one than that of preservation: it was of co-operating with evolution to bring about the New Age of the Aryan

Superman"

Gerald Suster

Author of *Hitler: Black Magician*

"You should create a higher body... You should create a creator. Let your hope be: may I bear the Superman!"

Friedrich Nietzsche

"A Folkish state must begin by raising marriage from the level of a continuous defilement of the race, and give it the consecration of an institution which is called upon to produce images of the Lord and not monstrosities halfway between man and ape"

Adolf Hitler

Thus, according to the Nazis, the Aryans are the "conquering and Master Race" of Nietzsche's prophecy, possessing the monopoly of beauty, intelligence and strength. Yet both Nietzsche and the Nazis admitted that such a race was "physiologically deteriorating", being continuously defiled *"through the democratic mingling of classes and races"* (118); by mixing with "lower races", the Aryan is threatened with disappearing from the surface of the planet... an alarming fact confirmed by today's ethnological maps of the world. Therefore, the immediate and most pressing concern is: how to preserve and increase the number of the last representatives of this glorious, Godlike race, a race destined to become the new ruling aristocracy of the earth, a race from which the Superman would spring? The only way to achieve this -according to Nietzsche and the Nazis- was through "continuous higher breeding" of the best elements of the best race on earth, ultimately leading to the creation of the Superman, the "masterpiece" of nature, for, as Nietzsche says, *"the goal is the Superman, not 'mankind'!"* (119)...*our way is upward, from the species across to the super-species"* (120)... Hitler, as Nietzsche, firmly believed that *"Man has to be passed and surpassed"*, culminating in the Superman, *"a new biological variety"*; the fact is that *"Man is becoming God... Man is God in the making... Gods and beasts, that is what our world is made of"* (121). Aryan man, being *"the highest image of the Lord"* (122), *"the only true species of man, the species with potential for evolution"*, the Fuehrer's task was hence much greater than preservation: it was that of *"co-operating with evolution"* to bring about *"the New Age of the Aryan Superman"* (123).

Nietzsche held that mankind should set as its highest goal the production of a "higher race" of Supermen, a race which, he stressed, should not come about as a result of chance or accident, but as the *conscious* and *artificial* product of human *will*, and, in the process, mankind should see to it that all "undesirables" -i.e. "degenerates" of the "lower order" who impede the evolution of humanity- are eliminated: this policy advocated by Nietzsche was none other "Eugenics", the radically racist program implemented by the Nazis that aimed at selecting and breeding the "best racial elements" who would represent a new superhuman species, thereby ensuring the evolution of humanity towards the God-Man: *"How many new gods are still possible!"* (124), wondered Nietzsche. Just like Plato's scheme for breeding the class of "Guardians" in the Republic, Nietzsche's coming Master Race would arise as a result of

"a fundamental, artificial and conscious breeding of … a higher type of dominating and Caesarian spirits" (125), for "the real issue is the production of the synthetic man… Lower men, the tremendous majority, are merely preludes and rehearsals out of whose medley the whole man appears here and there, the milestone man who indicates how far humanity has advanced so far" (126).

Contemplating the dedication of whole regions of the earth to human breeding experiments, to international racial unions, in order to end the "gruesome dominion of chance and nonsense" that has hitherto been called "history", Nietzsche sought

"to teach man the future of man as his will, as dependent on a human will, and to prepare for great enterprises and collective experiments in discipline and breeding" (127).

Hitler also believed that not wishful thinking but willed determination and discipline would achieve the "sacred duty" of *"making people stop talking superficially of God's will and actually fulfil God's will, and not let God's word be desecrated"* (128), "God's will" being none other than the preservation and breeding of Aryan Man… The Nazis were determined to create Nietzsche's "Master Race" of Supermen through the implementation of scientific breeding programs, the SS racial elite being chosen as the vehicle through which the racial purity of Germany would be re-established; for the foundation of the "Thousand-year Reich", the "New Order", Heinrich Himmler, through *Auslese* ("selection") and *Zucht* ("breeding"), *"wanted to cultivate a new human type- a loyal, duty-committed, tough, and self-sacrificing warrior, leader, scholar, and administrator all in one"* (129).

Creating the Master Race requires the implementation of "positive" as well as "negative" Eugenics, the former being a biological and moral breeding process and the latter, measures aimed at the sterilisation or elimination of *Lebensunwertiges Lebens* ("lives unworthy of life")... An essential part of "positive Eugenics" was marriage, which, in the noble sense, is an essential institution for breeding; Nietzsche saw that

> *"in marriage in the aristocratic, old aristocratic sense of the word it was a question of the breeding of a race" (130)... you should build beyond yourself. But first you must be built yourself, square-built in body and soul... You should create a higher body... You should create a creator. Let you hope be: 'May I bear the Superman!' " (131).*

Such a "racial" conception of marriage reminds us of the Nazi theories of *Rassenhygiene* ("racial hygiene") and programs of "positive Eugenics" encouraging large families among Aryan couples, especially the SS, who personified Aryanism, and whose members were ordered to "produce children of good blood" through a union with racially pure women, whether through marriage or outside marriage. Such was the principal task of the *Lebensborn* ("Spring of Life") program, a "breeding institution" created by Himmler

> *"as part of his plan 'to breed the SS into a biological elite, ... [a] racial nucleus from which Germany could replenish an Aryan inheritance now dangerously diluted through generations of race-mixing' " (132).*

In addition to offering welfare assistance and extending maternity and child-care facilities to SS families, *Lebensborn* also engaged in the abduction of children from countries occupied by Germany who were *"deemed to exhibit Aryan characteristics"*, and who were

> *"returned to 'the Fatherland' where they were to be 'Germanised' within 'racially acceptable families'. Such were the means adopted to create 'a community of physically and psychically homogeneous creatures' " (133).*

The Nazi project, then, resting on positive, conscious, scientific, and artificial breeding practices, was *"not so much Darwinian or social Darwinist as a vision of absolute control over the evolutionary process, over the biological human future"*. The Nazis, extensively using the Darwinian term "selection", *"sought to take over the functions of nature (natural selection) and God (the Lord giveth and the Lord taketh away) in orchestrating their own 'selections', their own version of human evolution"* (134) in order to produce a higher species of Man. What could be more Nietzschean?

As regards "negative Eugenics", or the darker side of the "god-forming" process leading to the Higher Man, Nietzsche -in theory- and the Nazis -in practice- showed a terrifying ruthlessness in their will to "eliminate" all "worthless" and "degenerate" creatures who represented the "greatest obstacle" to the divine mission assigned to humanity: the production of the Superman. Nothing should stand in the way of the perfect man; therefore, compulsory measures ranging from the sterilisation to the extermination of "sub-humans" were actively advocated by Nietzsche and implemented by the Nazis: *"are you a man who ought to desire a child? Are you the victor, the self-conqueror, the ruler of your sense, the lord of your virtues?"* (135), asked Nietzsche, restricting marriage to higher men, the only men deemed worthy of pro-creating, for *"the Biblical prohibition of life to decadents"* is: *'Thou shalt not procreate!'* " (136)... In a similar fashion, Hitler restricted the right to bear children to strong and healthy couples:

> *"a folkish state must begin by raising marriage from the level of a continuous defilement of the race, and give it the consecration of an institution which is called upon to produce images of the Lord and not monstrosities halfway between man and ape (137)... The Voelkish state must see to it that only the healthy beget children... Here the state must act as the guardian of a millennial future... It must put the most modern medical means in the service of this knowledge. It must declare unfit for propagation all who are in any way visibly sick or who have inherited a disease and can therefore pass it on" (138).*

As guardian of the "millennial future" that awaited Aryan humanity, the Third Reich made sure that the right to procreate was not granted to "unfit" parents, by implementing a whole panoply of measures designed to promote "racial hygiene", measures such as the coercive sterilisation or extermination of the "social degenerates" (homosexuals, criminals), the "hereditary ill" (the mentally or physically handicapped), as well as the Jews and other "lower races". By adopting the policy of "Euthanasia" or direct medical "mercy killing" of "life unworthy of life", the Nazis were only putting into practice what Nietzsche had so clearly advocated, namely *"the annihilation of millions of failures* (139). Nietzsche, in his determination to breed a race of Masters, in fact went much farther than calling for the mere restriction of marriage to Higher Men; he specifically predicted that *"the weak and the failures shall perish... And they shall be given every possible assistance"* (140). That prophecy was fulfilled a few decades later by Nietzsche's faithful disciples, the Nazis...

Essential to the breeding of a "higher humanity" (which is *the* central theme in Nietzsche's philosophy) is the concept of racial purity... A "Master Race" will only remain so if it preserves its purity, which is also its strength. Thus, in clear contrast to claims made by scholars like Hollingdale, Bluhm and Kaufmann, that Nietzsche saw culture as a product of racial mixture, the following statements leave no doubt as to his contempt for the "weak" and "worthless" mixed races, which he equates with mixed classes (the "masters" and the "slaves" being two distinct classes *as well as* races):

"The man of an era of dissolution which mixes the races together and who therefore contains within him the inheritance of a diversified descent... such a man of late cultures and broken lights will, on average, be a rather weak man: his fundamental desire is that the war which he is should come to an end (141) ... Our Europe of today, the scene of a senselessly sudden attempt at radical class- and consequently race- mixture, is as a result sceptical from top to bottom (142) ... Such a feeling of depression... may be the result of the crossing of too heterogeneous races (or of classes-genealogical and racial differences are also brought out in the classes: the European 'Weltschmerz,' the 'Pessimism' of the nineteenth century, is really the result of an absurd and sudden class-mixture" (143).

Denouncing *"the mad and fascinating semi-barbarism into which Europe has been plunged through the democratic mingling of classes and races"* (144), Nietzsche affirms that

"crossed races always mean at the same time crossed cultures, crossed moralities: they are usually more evil, crueller, more restless.... races that have become pure have always become stronger and more beautiful.- The Greeks offer us the model of a race and culture that has become pure: and hopefully we shall one day also achieve a pure European race and culture" *(145).*

The only racial mixture which was not complete anathema to Nietzsche is the one between European races (a mixture which would achieve the "pure European race"), for the latter were -in comparison with non-whites-the "higher races" of mankind, their jewel being the Aryan race, the only "conquering and Master Race" whose "physiological deterioration" (through intermixture with non-Aryan European races, namely the Alpine and Mediterranean races) Nietzsche strongly resented, for it gave way to the predominance of the *"short-skulled, dark-haired, pre-Aryan subject race"* (146). Nietzsche therefore believed that the Aryan Master Race should remain pure and untainted by the blood of 'lower races'. Indeed, just as members of a higher class should not mix with members of a lower class, so should members of a "higher race" abstain from mixing with those of a "lower race"; in Nietzsche's view, the chasm separating "Masters" and "Slaves" should never be bridged, for that transgresses nature's will, the natural order of things... When Nietzsche recommends the establishment of "international racial unions", he clearly restricts these unions to "higher" or aristocratic races, i.e. to members of the 'international' Aryan race, who are scattered all over the world...

Strikingly similar to Nietzsche's logic, the Nazi Eugenics program also focused on "the purification of the Aryan race"; indeed, racial purity was the dominant theme in the propaganda of the Third Reich. Hitler never claimed that the Germans were a pure race, yet he hoped that, through an intensive breeding scheme, they would "recover" their predominantly Nordic character in 200 years. According to Hitler, the Aryans are

"the highest species of humanity on earth" and will remain so if they "occupy themselves not merely with the breeding of dogs, horses and cats but also with care for the purity of their own blood" (147).

They should therefore refrain from mixing with "lesser races", for *"the result of all racial crossing is... always the following: (a) Lowering of the level of the higher race; (b) Physical and intellectual regression and hence the beginning of a slowly but surely progressing sickness (148)* ... Indeed, racial mixture is the worst "curse" that could befall any breeding scheme aimed at producing a "higher humanity":

"No more than Nature desires the mating of weaker with stronger individuals, even less does she desire the blending of a higher with a lower race, since, if she did, her whole work of higher breeding, over perhaps hundreds of thousands of years, might be ruined with one blow" (149).

Therefore, the greatest "crime against humanity" in Nazi Germany was race mixing between Aryans and non-Aryans, for this violated the aristocratic principle of nature, i.e. the unalterable, inalienable inequality between the "Masters" and the "slaves".

The State as an agency for breeding the universal Master Race

"The state is the coldest of all cold monsters... Many too are born: the state was invented for the many-too-many... There, where the state ceases-look there, my brothers, do you not see it: the rainbow and the bridges to the Superman?"

Friedrich Nietzsche

"... the current monstrosity of human mechanism now called state"

Adolf Hitler

"A herd of blonde beasts of prey, a race of conquerors and masters, which with all its warlike organisation and all its organising power pounces with its terrible claws on a population, in numbers possibly tremendously superior, but as yet formless, as yet nomad. Such is the origin of the 'state'."

"The state is not the highest end of man... Higher men should gain great influence in the state because they are allowed to consider it as a means, whereas all the others under the sway of those unconscious purposes of the state are themselves only means for the fulfilment of the State-purpose."

"The maintenance of the military state is the last means of all of acquiring or maintaining the great tradition with regard to the supreme type of man, the strong type. And all concepts that perpetuate enmity and difference in rank between states (e.g. nationalism, protective tariffs) may appear sanctioned in this light"

Friedrich Nietzsche

"The state represents no end, but a means to an end. Its end lies in the development of the race's spiritual and ideal abilities leading to the formation of a higher culture... States which do not serve this purpose are misbegotten, monstrosities in fact"

"The mission of the German people on earth is that of assembling and preserving the most valuable stocks of basic racial elements in the Aryan people and raising them to a dominant position"

Adolf Hitler

Racial purity, along with other "positive" as well as "negative" eugenics measures, could only be achieved and preserved as part of a thorough and select breeding scheme; the "Master Race" of Nietzsche's prophecy would only arise out of conscious human will and determination... By specifically mentioning that this breeding would consist of "conscious", "artificial", and "organised" experiments to end the "gruesome dominion of chance and nonsense", Nietzsche clearly had in mind some sort of mechanism, a means through which this "disciplined" process would take place. In other words, only the apparatus, organisation, and institutions of a state could ensure the implementation of such a project... Yet the sole purpose of such a "state" would be the breeding of the Superman; any other type of state -which was not a means to a great end, but a purposeless entity- was dismissed by Nietzsche as a monstrosity; in fact, he held the modern Liberal state -whose only function was the protection of "life, liberty, and property"- in utter contempt, for it represented the institution of the many, of the unfree, of the herd:

> *"Now I shall speak to you of the death of peoples. The state is the coldest of all cold monsters... Many too are born: the state was invented for the many-too-many! ... My brothers, do you want to suffocate in the fumes of their animal mouths and appetites? Better to break the window and leap into the open air. Avoid this bad odour! Leave the idolatry of the superfluous!" (150).*

Only where *this* state ceases, does the man with a great soul, *"the man who is not superfluous"*, begin: only where the purposeless state ceases, do *"the rainbow and the bridges to the Superman"* appear (151).

When Nietzsche declares that *"culture and the state... are antagonists.... that which is great in the cultural sense has been unpolitical, even anti-political"* (152), he is referring to the Liberal idea of the state, as opposed to the classic Platonic conception of the state and politics which he praises in his early writings (*The Birth of Tragedy* and *The Greek State*) as a means to the production of great human beings. Indeed, Nietzsche argues that the modern philosophy of the state *"stems from the 'liberal optimistic view of the world' which has its roots in the doctrines of French Rationalism and the French Revolution"*... Scorning modern politics, whose goal *"is to free the state from the possibility of the incalculable convulsions of war and establish it on a purely rational basis for the pursuit of economic ends"*, Nietzsche condemns Liberalism's *"deviation of the state-tendency into a money-tendency"*, into a *"selfish state-less money aristocracy"* (153). Nietzsche's anti-political and anti-statist philosophy should therefore only be understood as an opposition to the liberal, democratic, and Christian state which, together with its *"imperfect manifestations"* such as the *"German [Second] Reich"*, he views as *"the decaying form of the state"* (154). Nietzsche did despise the Second

Reich, yet not because of its authoritarian character; quite the contrary, he despised the "new Reich" because it was not authoritarian and elitist enough, being *"founded on the most threadbare and despised ideas: equal rights and universal suffrage"* (155).

Equally adamant in their opposition to the idea of state idolatry were the Nazis, contrary to the opinion of some scholars (like Kaufmann) who have failed to draw the essential difference between the two totalitarian ideologies of Nazism and Fascism, which lies in their theory of the state, and who therefore tend to confuse them. While Fascism venerates the state, viewing it as an end in itself, National Socialism, like Nietzsche, venerates the "Master Race", and *not* the state, teaching that the latter is no end in itself, but is merely a vehicle for the selection and the preservation of the best racial elements of the nation. The state therefore only has value if it contributes to the enhancement of the human species; in this respect, the Nazis were as firm as Nietzsche in their condemnation of the Liberal state which is devoid of any higher purpose. Hitler in fact held in utter contempt *"the current monstrosity of human mechanism now called state"* (156), whose role is restricted to the mere preservation of peace and order...

The state being no end in itself, it must be in the service of higher cultural and spiritual ends. Politics should therefore be subservient to culture. It is in this sense that Nietzsche considered himself "anti-political". Declaring that *"the state is not the highest end of man"*, Nietzsche criticises the *"Hegelian tendency"* which he believes has led to the modern *"apotheosis of the state"* (157), and concludes that only the higher men should rule, for they are the only individuals who are able to use the state for the fulfilment of higher ends:

> *"Such men should gain great influence in the State because they are allowed to consider it as a means, whereas all the others under the sway of those unconscious purposes of the State are themselves only means for the fulfilment of the State-purpose" (158).*

Nietzsche's anti-political and anti-statist stance is hence not absolute, i.e. it is not an opposition to *all* types of politics or to *all* types of states, but only to the Liberal view of political life; this point seems to have been missed by scholars like Kaufmann, whose one-sided, superficial analysis of Nietzschean thought ignored the strikingly clear political character of many of Nietzsche's writings which are an apology of the war-like hierarchical state, the latter acting as a breeding agency for the Superman:

"A herd of blonde beasts of prey, a race of conquerors and masters, which with all its warlike organisation and all its organising power pounces with its terrible claws on a population, in numbers possibly tremendously superior, but as yet formless, as yet nomad. Such is the origin of the 'state'" (159)...

"Organised beasts of prey": this specific quotation implies that Nietzsche means that even the Master Race must have some kind of framework or "Aristocratic government" (the SS order?) of "pure masters" (racially pure?) in order to defeat inferior peoples. Praising the state as *"organised immorality"*, as *"Will to Power, to war, to conquest, to revenge"* (160), Nietzsche leaves no doubt as to his advocacy of a radically authoritarian, elitist -and even nationalist!- type of government as the only means to the breeding and preservation of a higher type of man:

"The maintenance of the military state is the last means of all of acquiring or maintaining the great tradition with regard to the supreme type of man, the strong type. And all concepts that perpetuate enmity and difference in rank between states (e.g., nationalism, protective tariffs) may appear sanctioned in this light" (161).

It is surprising that such crucial statements should be overlooked by prominent Nietzsche scholars like Kaufmann and Hollingdale, hastily reaching the conclusion that Nietzsche was *absolutely* anti-statist...

The Nazis, like Nietzsche, perceived the state as a means to a higher end, namely that of breeding the Master Race; the state was merely an agent of the race, and thus it was the racial Nazi worldview which would determine the actions of the state:

"One can speak of the Nazi state as a 'biocracy'... a cure through purification and revitalization of the Aryan race... Just as in a theocracy, the state itself is no more than a vehicle for the divine purpose, so in the Nazi biocracy was the state no more than a means to achieve 'a mission of the German people on earth': that of 'assembling and preserving the most valuable stocks of basic racial elements in this [Aryan} people... [and] raising them to a dominant position" (162).

It is as if the Nazis had formed the SS state to actualise Nietzsche's call for the breeding of Supermen in body and soul. Hitler believed that the state should assume not only the preservation of the race, but also *"the development of its spiritual and ideal abilities"* leading to *"the formation of a higher culture... States which do not serve this purpose are misbegotten, monstrosities in fact"* (163). The breeding of the Master Race -according to the Nietzschean and Nazi doctrines- transcends by far the idolatry of the state, yet state institutions are needed for the fulfilment of this sacred mission of mankind, which could only be actualised if it becomes the noblest and highest -indeed the *only*- purpose of the state...

Based on the aforementioned statements, it is safe to draw the conclusion that when Nietzsche labels the state the "coldest of cold monsters" and when he dissociates politics from culture, he is referring to the modern Liberal state and democratic government, *not* to the classic Platonic state and Politics whose highly authoritarian, elitist and ethical character as well as cultural and spiritual purpose Nietzsche held in the highest praise, as opposed to what he disdainfully terms "petty politics", i.e. the Liberal-humanist, egalitarian and secular nature of today's purposeless 'minimal' state, whose main function -indeed *only* function- lies in preserving and protecting the "petty values and virtues" of "petty people", namely "Life, Liberty, Property, and the pursuit of happiness", the "green-pasture happiness" of "herd-animals"... Confident that "petty politics" and the 'minimal state', which are based on the hedonistic philosophy of comfort and ease, could only produce mediocrity and never create culture and greatness, Nietzsche proudly proclaimed that *"the time for petty politics is over"* and that the next century *"will bring with it the fight for the dominion of the earth- the compulsion to great politics"* (164).

Great Politics: the rule of the Aryan universal Master Race

"The Masters of the earth... a higher kind of man who, thanks to their superiority in will, riches, and influence, employ democratic Europe as their most pliant and supple instrument for getting hold of the destinies of the earth, so as to work as artists upon 'man' himself... The time is coming when politics will have a different meaning"

"The Superman is the meaning of the earth. Let your will say: the Superman shall be the meaning of the earth"

Friedrich Nietzsche

"... a peace, supported not by the palm branches of tearful, pacifist female mourners, but based on the victorious sword of a master people, putting the world into the service of a higher culture"

Adolf Hitler

"I write for a species of man that does not yet exist: for the 'Masters of the

earth'"

Friedrich Nietzsche

"Physically and mentally the Aryans are pre-eminent among all peoples, for that reason they are by right... the lords of the world"
Houston Steward Chamberlain

"O my brothers, your nobility shall not gaze backward, but outward! You shall be fugitives from all fatherlands and fore-fatherlands!"
Friedrich Nietzsche

"The concept of nation has become meaningless... The New Order cannot be conceived in terms of the national boundaries of the peoples with an historic past, but in terms of race that transcends these boundaries. France carried her great revolution beyond her borders with the conception of nation. With the conception of race, National Socialism will carry its revolution abroad and recast the world... The day will come when even here in Germany what is known as 'nationalism' will practically have ceased to exist. What will take place in the world will be a universal society of Masters and over-Lords"

Adolf Hitler

In contrast to the Liberal or bourgeois conception of politics which gives the state no other function than to serve people's "animal desires and appetites", Nietzsche advances his own radically anti-democratic conception of politics, "great politics", i.e. a "Higher Politics" which does not separate between the "temporal" and the "spiritual" -as the modern secular state does- but rather puts the "political" in the service of the "spiritual", entrusting the state with a holy mission: that of breeding the future *"masters of the earth"*,

"a higher kind of man who, thanks to their superiority in will, knowledge, riches, and influence, employ democratic Europe as their most pliant and supple instrument for getting hold of the destinies of the earth, so as to work as artists upon 'man' himself... The time is coming when politics will have a different meaning".

"Great politics" will indeed be different, for it will witness the coming to power of a *"new, tremendous aristocracy"* which will be made up of *"philosophical men of power and artist-tyrants"* (165); in other words, the rule of Plato's class of Guardians... Great men are above politics:

"The highest men live beyond the rulers, freed from all bonds, and in the rulers they have their instruments" (166).

There lies their greatness, Nietzsche asserts, but also their misfortune: *"the most unpardonable thing about you: you have the power and you will not rule"* (167)... So, Nietzsche held, in order to restore human greatness, the future should be different; the "highest men" *should* and *shall* also be the leaders, the rulers:

"The best shall rule, the best wants to rule!... The highest man should also be the highest lord on earth", for "there is no harder misfortune in all human destiny than when the powerful of the earth are not also the first men. Then everything becomes false and awry and monstrous" (168).

Justice itself commands that the best should also be the first, and they will: "let your will say: the Superman *shall* be the meaning of the earth!" (169).

To establish "great politics", or the rule of the Superman, Nietzsche argues, conscious and willed determination, as well as organised action, are needed; but it is only war, the holiest and noblest of wars, that would actualise this dream; history indeed teaches that all great events and creations are the product of struggle and violence:

"A dominating race can grow up only out of terrible and violent beginnings. Problem: where are the barbarians of the twentieth century?" (170).

These barbarians who, as Prometheus, *"come from the heights"*, are *"a species of conquering and ruling natures in search of material to mould"* (171). Nietzsche leaves us no reason to believe -as Kaufmann does- that his "great politics" and his "war" of the future are only spiritual: what Nietzsche means by "war" is actually a *real* war *as well as* a spiritual one, all in the service of the highest cause and *only* truth, that of breeding a new species, the Superman, a cause and a truth that require the complete -and violent- elimination of all Judaeo-Christian values and "millennial lie" which form the basis of Western civilisation:

"When truth steps into battle with the lie of millennia we shall have convulsions, an earthquake spasm, a transposition of valley and mountain such as has never been dreamed of. The concept politics has then become completely absorbed into a war of spirits, all the power-structures of the old society have been blown into the air- they one and all reposed on the lie: there will be wars such as there have never yet been on earth. Only

after me will there be grand politics on earth" (172).

Nietzsche in fact associates great politics in *Beyond Good and Evil* with "blood and iron", *"which was Bismarck's metonym for military might"*... There is therefore

"strong evidence for the conclusion that the great politics of the future, which is integrally related to Nietzsche's revaluation of all values, is also a politics of the real world.... there is every reason to believe that 'all power structures of the old society' will be 'exploded' in fact and not just in thought" (173).

"Great politics" is indeed the Will to Power elevated from the personal level to the macro-level, to the political level... And here is where the Nazis excelled as faithful disciples of Nietzsche: by perceiving "politics" as only the outward manifestation, the practical, fragmentary and temporary application of a religious vision of the universe, as the pillar for new values and the means towards the ultimate goal and destiny of humanity, namely the breeding and world rule of the Aryan Master Race, viewed by Chamberlain -and later by Hitler- as the "Lords of the earth":

"In his Politics Aristotle writes: 'If there were men who in physical stature alone were so pre-eminent as the representatives of the Gods, then every one would admit that other men by right must be subject unto them. If this, however, is true in reference to the body, then there is still greater justification for distinguishing between pre-eminent and commonplace souls'. Physically and mentally the Aryans are pre-eminent among all peoples; for that reason they are by right, as the Stagirite expresses himself, the lords of the world" (174).

Thus did Hitler call for *"a peace, supported not by the palm branches of tearful, pacifist female mourners, but based on the victorious sword of a master people, putting the world into the service of a higher culture" (175).* For Nietzsche and the Nazis, "great politics" -i.e. *real* politics; the only one which history records- meant no less than the projection of the Will to Power on a world scale, the fight for the dominion of the earth by a race of Supermen, a goal which soon became the cornerstone of the Third Reich's foreign policy ... The concept of race is indeed universal, transcending the political boundaries of states and nations; yet this "universalism" professed by Nietzsche and the Nazis is in no way a prelude and a longing for a universalistic-humanist or internationalist-pacifist ideal! It is rather an integral feature of their characteristic "racist-aristocratic worldview" whose ultimate goal is a world dominated by the "Master Race" (a term which is Nietzschean as well as Nazi) of distinct morality and kind, which transcends the political, geographical, linguistic, and cultural boundaries of nation-states.

Nietzsche's supra-statist and supra-nationalist thought emanates from the very essence of his racialist-eugenicist philosophy dominated by the will to breed a new universal race of masters, a distinct species of born-leaders destined to rule the earth:

"I write for a species of man that does not yet exist: for the 'masters of the earth' " (176).

These "masters of the earth" do not belong exclusively to one nation, rather they can be found in several nations; therefore, in order to fulfil their sacred mission, their allegiance should be *only* to their race, the Master Race, and *not* to the particular nation or culture they belong to:

"O my brothers, your nobility shall not gaze backward, but outward! You shall be fugitives from all fatherlands and fore-fatherlands!" (177).

In order to meet the challenges of the Great Politics of the future, which will be radically aristocratic and supra-national, witnessing "great wars of the spirit" at the scale of the entire globe, members of the Aryan "Master Race" -who are scattered all over the earth- should give up traditional or "narrow" nationalism in favour of a universal "racist-aristocratic" view of the world which would serve to unite and organise them in preparation for their world conquest and enslavement of "lower races"... The conflict between "Masters" and "slaves", between "Supermen" and "sub-humans", is indeed an international one... Nietzsche was calling for some sort of "aristocratic world government" led by a superior "universal class", a distinct race endowed with incomparable physical, mental and moral strength, a nobility of blood and spirit.

This prophecy soon came to be realised by the S.S., a fiercely international -yet rigorously Nordic- Order of carefully selected "Aryan Supermen" in body and spirit, whose ultimate goal was the establishment of the "S.S. state" in Europe, a blueprint for world rule by an "Aryan universal aristocracy". The Nazis, for whom the Master Race was an international aristocratic concept, proved themselves true Nietzscheans in their transcendence of nation-states. The "Black Order" (i.e. the S.S. state) was a racially structured and hierarchical organisation that represented a radical alternative not only to the Liberal-humanitarian concept of

Western civilisation, but also to the current idea of the national state. The racist-international membership of the S.S. organisation was a living proof that Nazism placed the concept of race above the concept of nation. Hitler was indeed absolutely convinced that racialism as a world-revolutionary principle would replace traditional nationalism and become the vehicle of history, ensuring the supremacy of the racially superior nations, i.e. the nations which would set as their highest goal the production of the Aryan Superman; herein lay the universal "world-historical" and "world-political" mission for Nazi Germany:

The conception of nation has become meaningless... The new order cannot be conceived in terms of the national boundaries of the peoples with an historic past, but in terms of race that transcend those boundaries. France carried her great Revolution beyond her borders with the conception of nation. With the conception of race, National Socialism will carry its revolution abroad and recast the world" (178).

The Nazi creed therefore put race above nation, for the Aryan Master Race is universal, its representative beings scattered all over the earth. Hitler made that point clear when he admitted that he

"had to encourage 'national' feelings for reasons of expediency; but I was already aware that the 'nation' idea could only have a temporary value. The day will come when even here in Germany what is known as 'nationalism' will practically have ceased to exist. What will take its place in the world will be a universal society of masters and over-lords" (179).

What could be more Nietzschean? Nazism put Nietzsche's theory in motion, and the SS institution was the vehicle through which Nietzsche's Universal Master Race would see the day.

Indeed, although Nazism originated in Germany and had clear nationalist overtones (Germany being considered as the spiritual Fatherland of all Aryans), it was nonetheless primarily a universal movement whose biological and moral-spiritual racism went far beyond both state and national idolatry, for racial boundaries clashed with national boundaries; this fact was overlooked by scholars like R.J. Hollingdale and Walter Kaufmann who have failed to draw the difference between racism and nationalism -which are two distinct, often conflicting doctrines-concluding that the Nazis' "national idolatry" was incompatible with Nietzsche's universal thought... In reply to such allegations, it should be noted that the Nazis were first and foremost racist, not nationalist, and their racist-aristocratic worldview was therefore supra-national, given the fact that nations comprise the most manifold racial types and are based on ethnic (mainly cultural, linguistic, historical) factors which do not determine moral, biological, and psychological -i.e. racial- superiority; nationality and language have little to do with race... According to the Nazi racial doctrine, an Italian, a Syrian, or an Iranian of Nordic race is superior to a German or a Swede of Alpine, Slavonic race. Indeed, the racist considers that race is above culture, for superiority is related to genes and *Geist* ("spirit"), which are innate, and not to language, culture and nationality, which are acquired. A true believer in the importance of race would in fact end up condemning modern states and nations, for these are "prisons of races" always racially heterogeneous (because of racial mixture) and based on cultural and historical bonds and experiences rather than deeper, more important and essential biological, moral and spiritual ties. Hence, political geography is entirely distinct from racial geography; nationality has no foundation in race (180).

Hitler, who declared that *"race does not lie in the language, but exclusively in the blood"* (181), was expressing the need to avoid the error of contemporary scholars who confuse community of language with identity of race, a "confusion" referred to by H.S. Chamberlain as utter "chaos"... Chamberlain cites as an example the case of the dark, short-skulled, broad-faced Alpine race, of Mongoloid origins and characteristics, which dominates in the Alps and Eastern Europe, an "un-Germanic", non-Aryan race which is nonetheless considered today "Germanic" simply because some of its members speak the German language:

> *"How could we then bring ourselves to regard those Europeans who are descended from this altogether un-Germanic type as 'Germanic', simply because they speak an Indo-European language and have assimilated Indo-European culture? I consider it, on the contrary, a most important duty to make a clear distinction here, if we wish to understand past and present history"* (182).

Another illustration to grasp the racial transcendence of nations, is Chamberlain's view of the Syrian (i.e. the Levantine):

> *"if we turn to a textbook of geography or an encyclopaedia, we shall find it stated that the present population of Syria is 'to the greatest extent Semitic'. This is false; just as false as the statement we find in the same sources, that the Armenians are 'Aryans'. Here again we see the widespread confusion of language and race; we should, on the same footing, logically have to*

maintain that the negroes of the United States were Anglo-Saxons...
The Syrian 'Semite' of today should be called Semite in language rather
than in race, and the so-called Aryan Armenian, of Phrygian origin, has
perhaps not 10 per cent of Indo-European blood in his vein" (183).

In fact, Greater Syria (i.e. the "Fertile Crescent", the Levant) has been
overrun and invaded by several races, including the Indo-Europeans (the
word "Syria" derives from the Sanskrit word *Surya*, i.e. the Aryan Vedic
Sun-god): as an example, Lebanon's population is a

"mixture of Mediterranean subtypes, admixed with some Alpine
and Nordic elements with here and there a faint trace of Negroid and
Mongoloid infusion" (184).

Thus, in this tiny country alone —as in most nations today- the most
manifold racial types could be found, ranging from the pure Nordic to the
pure Semite... All these examples serve to prove the fact that racism is
distinct from -even antithetical to- nationalism. The Nazi creed was racist
and therefore supra-national, quite similar to Nietzsche's thought; that
point seems to have been overlooked by Kaufmann and Hollingdale...

As a result of the continuous migrations and invasions over the
centuries, the "Aryan conquering and Master Race" which invaded the
whole of Europe, America, and parts of Asia, mixing with non-Aryans,
has become a "universal race", its representatives being found in most
nations, which contain Aryan as well as other blood, from America to
Afghanistan... In this respect, the Nazi concept of "Master Race" was
identical to Nietzsche's, being universal in character, not restricted to the
mere Germans. Indeed, in Mein Kampf, Hitler speaks of "the Aryans"
as the Master Race, not just the Germans (at least half the Germans are
not Aryans), and Chamberlain praises *Der Germane* ("the Teuton", i.e. the
Nordic), not just *Der Deutsche* ("the German"). According to Nazism, all
regions of the globe where the Aryan expanded, settled, or mixed with
other peoples, could be considered as having potential Aryan blood (blood
which should be "Germanised", i.e. Aryanised, and brought back to the
German Fatherland); in this regard, the Nazis planned to extend the
Third Reich's political influence to Persia, Tibet, and India, the original
homeland and cradle of the Aryan race... The Germanic invasions of
Russia, Italy, Greece, Syria, Persia, India, etc... have made boundaries
between nations obsolete from the racial perspective.

The Aryan is potentially everywhere, and racial inter-mixture has not led to his disappearance: rather, in some nations, he dominated the natives and kept his blood nearly pure, and in other places he mixed with - and was overwhelmed by- other races; as an example, the Aryans who invaded Russia mixed with the Mongols, producing the "inferior" Slavs of today, who are of Alpine, Eurasian race, i.e. mere "blond Mongols" despised by the Nazis as *Untermenschen* ("sub-humans") and *Menschentiere* ("human beasts")... Yet, despite this mixture, one could still find today, among the predominantly East-Baltic, Slavic population of Russia, some representatives of the Aryan race... Herein lies the universality of race, which is above nation and culture: an Aryan Russian is therefore -according to the Nazi racial doctrine- superior to an Alpine German. Aryans could thus be found all over the world precisely because of their expansionism: what is needed is just racial consciousness in order to unite them according to criteria defined by the "Nuremberg racial laws of nationality" in 1935, which gave a "certificate of Aryanism" to any person exhibiting Nordic features and morality (a certificate which entitled him to acquire German nationality upon his request!), and which withheld nationality from all non-Aryans. Indeed, the preamble to the said laws clearly stipulates that nationality in the new Reich will be based solely on a person's race: *"Only members of the race may be citizens of the state"*.

Nazism was therefore an Aryan -not just a German- movement aimed at launching and establishing an international Aryan revolution and world rule, a movement uniting all Aryans and determined to carry out the "racial cleansing" or forced purification of nations which contained Nordic blood (or, as in the case of Russia, where "Slavic blood" was largely predominant, to enslave these "lower races" and "Germanise" the few Aryans among them). The Aryan "Superman" is everywhere; no boundaries should separate him from his brothers in race. States and nations are his enemies, for they are artificial, non-racial entities which he should seek to transcend in order to establish the rule of the Master Race. Nazism was thus a "racist-aristocratic" international movement quite distinct from Socialist or Liberal internationalism, and based on the rule of the Higher Race. We are not far from Nietzsche's "great politics" and its world rule by a universal "Master Race"... The extensive argumentation on the widespread confusion between "race" and "nation" and the racist-aristocratic nature of Nazism leads us to the following conclusion: the SS, Nazi Germany's aristocracy, were the embodiment of Nietzsche's universal Master Race: a nationally heterogeneous body (including members recruited from over 17 nations) yet with racially homogeneous members selected according to specific higher biological and moral qualities, a universal race of Supermen in body and soul: in other words, Nietzsche's thought put into motion, his words transformed into deeds...

Thus, the argument of Hollingdale and Kaufmann, that the Nazis worshipped the state or the nation, becomes obsolete. In fact, even the nationalist aspect of Nazism -which was a far cry from the "bourgeois nationalism" based on mere language, not race, and thus despised by Hitler - was universal in character, for its "mystical racism" called for the establishment of a supra-national, mystical-racist "Germanic Reich" (185) across Europe ("from the Atlantic to the Urals"), extending even to the Middle East, central and South-West Asia (to include all former "Aryan nations" such as Persia, India, ...), an Aryan empire whose core would be Germany. Nazism espoused "racist nationalism", a unique doctrine in the fact that it combined nationalism and racism, these two often conflicting doctrines. The ultimate goal of *Der Voelkische Staat* (The "racial" or "racist" state) was to achieve a racially pure nation, a nation based on race, and thus to reconcile race and nation. Germany was the perfect nation for the achievement of that ambitious project, for it was the original home (*Urheimat*) of the ancient Germanic tribes of pure Aryan blood, direct descendants of the original Indo-Europeans, and so it should become the "universal state" for all Aryans of the world who would be entitled to German nationality (ironically, Israel, the nation of all the world's Jews, whom the Nazis despised as "typical sub-humans", is a sort of Semitic religious version of Nazi Germany's Aryan racist nationalism...).

It is an undeniable fact that the Nazis were nationalists, yet their nationalism sprung from their racism, which praised Germany as a truly "Aryan nation"; their universal esoteric doctrine was therefore compatible with their nationalist exoteric doctrine, and there lies the uniqueness of the Nazi doctrine... The mystical Aryan racism of the Nazi creed transcended Germany but did not deny its huge Aryan spiritual and racial heritage. Hitler -as Nietzsche- indeed used "race" and "nation" interchangeably, reflecting his doctrine's racial dimension to the word "nation" which, together with the word "Volk" (people or race), had the deepest spiritual meaning to the Nazis, namely

"the union of a group of people with a transcendental 'essence'...[which] might be called 'nature' or 'cosmos' or 'mythos', but in each instance... was fused to man's inmost nature, and represented the source of his creativity, his depth of feeling, his individuality, and his unity with other members of the Volk" (186).

Significantly, Nietzsche's thought, although definitely supra-national and racist-international, was also not as anti-German as scholars like Walter Kaufmann, R.J. Hollingdale, and William Bluhm would like us to believe: the "hatred" he shows for the Germans in some of his writings is more of a disappointed hope and resentment directed against the "un-Germanic" racially mixed, Christian, Liberal and democratic modern Germans, deploring what he calls the "domestication" of the "splendid blond Teuton beast":

"The Germans may well be the most mixed of all peoples... Let anyone look upon the face of the Germans. Everything that had manly, exuberant blood in it went abroad (187)... Who has not pondered sadly over what the German spirit could be! But this nation has deliberately made itself stupid, for practically a thousand years: nowhere else are the two great European narcotics, alcohol and Christianity, so viciously abused" (188).

Contrasting these "un-Germanic" Germans of today (*Die Deutschen*) with the ancient pure Germanic tribes (*Die Germanen*), Nietzsche held the latter in the highest praise, admiring their war-like nature and manliness, and sadly acknowledging the fact that the number of the pure representatives of this strong race in Germany is continuously dwindling. Still, in spite of their weaknesses, the Germans remained, in the eyes of Nietzsche (and the Nazis, of course),

"the most hopeful stuff out of which to make Supermen... at the core of this German race is to be found a fine blond strength, a capacity for disciplined obedience, for efficient cooperation, an energy that can be stimulated into Dionysian activity and enjoyment, a noble discontent with the world as it is. Even the German search for 'depth' is a sign of the German Will to Power".

Nietzsche indeed proudly declared: *"Wir Deutschen wollen etwas von uns, was man von uns doch nicht wollte- wir wollen etwas mehr"* (189) ("We Germans want something from ourselves, which no one has yet wanted of us- we want something more"). Even today's mixed and Christianised Germans still possessed, in Nietzsche's opinion, *"more manly virtues than any other country of Europe can exhibit"* (190). The modern German is still relatively the best representative of the "Goths" and the "Vandals", the "Aryan conquering and Master Race":

"The profound, icy mistrust which the German provokes, as soon as he

113

arrives at power, – even at the present time, is always still an aftermath of that inextinguishable horror with which for whole centuries Europe has regarded the wrath of the blonde Teuton beast" (191).

Indeed, Nietzsche asks, *"must not our actual German word gut mean 'the Godlike', the man of Godlike race? And be identical with the national name (originally the noble's name) of the Goths?"* (192). What better statement could prove that Nietzsche considered -as did the Nazis- that the ancient Germans belonged to the Godlike Master Race? It is quite incredible that prominent Nietzsche scholars could disregard such statements of crucial importance, which show Nietzsche's undeniable admiration for the Germans, ancient as well as modern...

Quite similarly to Nietzsche, the Nazis considered the Germans "a master race" belonging to the wider "Aryan Master Race". Hitler never denied the fact that the Germans were a mixed race whose Nordic blood did not exceed 40 per cent of the population: *"Our German nationality, unfortunately, is no longer based on a unified racial nucleus"* (193), yet he still thought of the Aryan Germans as a higher race. The mission of Nazi Germany was indeed to purify the German people of non-Nordic elements through positive and negative Eugenics, in the hope of turning them into relatively pure Aryans in a period not exceeding 200 year. In other words, to bring back the predominance in Germany of Nietzsche's much-admired "Goths", a race that would "Germanise" –i.e. Aryanise- Europe -racially, culturally and spiritually- all over again as it did centuries ago, thus realising the Nazi dream of a "Germanic Europe" quite in line with Nazism's supra-national "racist nationalism", for Hitler considered that Germany will only truly be Germany when it will become Europe.

CHAPTER FIVE

ANTI-SEMITISM: THE JEW AS
THE SUPREME DECADENT

Racist-Aristocratic anti-Semitism versus Christian anti-Semitism

"People of the basest origin, in part rabble, outcasts not only from good but also from respectable society, raised away from even the smell of culture, without discipline, without knowledge, without the remotest suspicion that there is such a thing as conscience in spiritual matters; simply— Jews"

"Ours is the kingdom of the rabble… Rabble, however, means hotchpotch. Rabble-hotchpotch: in that everything is mixed up with everything else, saint and scoundrel and gentleman and Jew and every beast out of Noah's ark"

"Decay! Decay! Ne'er sank the world so low! Rome is now a harlot and a brothel, too, Rome's Caesar a beast, and God himself- a Jew!"

Friedrich Nietzsche

"In contrast to the noble, creative, and constructive Nordic, the Jew is ignoble, parasitic, and destructive"

Alfred Rosenberg

"The Jew is alien to our civilisation, unfitted by his very 'brain convolutions' from entering fully into the current of life about him!"

Houston Stewart Chamberlain

"Was er glaubt is einerlei, die Rasse ist die Schweinerei" (*"it's not the faith that they embrace, the swinishness is in the race"*)

Nazi anti-Semitic slogan

Anti-Semitism - i.e. hostility to the Jews, who are considered the typical representatives of the Semitic race and spirit - lies at the heart of the Nazi doctrine, constituting one of its most characteristic features. Indeed, Alfred Rosenberg, the official philosopher of the Third Reich, asserted that the "subhuman" and "degenerate" Jew was the perfect antithesis to the Aryan "Superman", the exact opposite of the Nordic in all respects:

"In contrast to the noble, creative, and constructive Nordic, he is ignoble, parasitic, and destructive" (1).

The Jew's very existence, according to Nazism, jeopardised human culture and progress. Yet anti-Semitism -of the fiercest kind- also clearly pervades Nietzsche's writings, forming an integral part and representing an essential characteristic of his philosophy, although some Jewish scholars (especially Walter Kaufmann and William Bluhm) chose to downplay his contempt for the Jews by simply disregarding the numerous passages in which he proves himself as virulent an anti-Semite as any good Nazi, while highlighting the very few citations where Nietzsche merely acknowledges the Jews' resilience and will to survival despite unfavourable or hostile conditions…

However, the anti-Semitism displayed in Nietzsche's writings and Nazi propaganda did not belong to the traditional Christian anti-Semitism prevailing in Germany at that time, and directed at the Jews mainly as a religious community. Rather, it was a far different and no doubt deeper racial, intellectual, moral, and metaphysical brand of anti-Semitism -what one might term "racist-aristocratic anti-Semitism" or "racist-spiritual anti-Semitism" (in opposition to Christian anti-Semitism)- which was totally in line with the Aryan paganism of both the Nietzschean and Nazi doctrines, and which went far beyond mere religious, cultural or social hatred of the Jews, targeting the "Jewish spirit"… i.e. condemning the very essence of Jewry, its moral and spiritual foundations… This explains why Nietzsche, a staunch (yet pagan, not Christian) anti-Semite himself, nonetheless denounced the "anti-Semites" of Germany, scorning them for being "self-styled Christians" who were unconscious of the fact that the Christianity they were so proud of, that religion they were so confidently using against the Jews, was nothing but the ultimate consequence of Judaism, its continuation and not its negation, as the following passage shows:

> *"The Jews are the most fateful nation in world history; their after-effect has falsified mankind to such an extent that today the Christian is able to feel anti-Jewish without realizing he is the ultimate consequence of the Jews"* (2).

The Nazis, too, were clearly not "Christian anti-Semites", their pagan racist worldview denouncing the Jews as a "degenerate, mixed race", not as a religious community, as shown by this blunt Nazi slogan: *"was er glaubt is einerlei, die Rasse is die Schweinerei"* ("It's not the faith that they embrace, the swinishness is in the race")… Thus was "the religion of race" more lethal than that of Christ or Mohammed (3). Hitler indeed stressed that the Jew *"has always been a people with definite racial characteristics and never a religion"* (4). The racial anti-Semitism which the Nazis espoused was thus inspired by H.S. Chamberlain, the racist philosopher who considered the Jew *"alien to our civilization, unfitted by is very 'brain convolutions' from entering fully into the current of the life about him!" (5).*

Yet this racial anti-Semitism also had a spiritual dimension: indeed, the Nazi esoteric doctrine, which viewed race as a mystic-biological concept, did not stop at merely condemning the Jew as a "racial degenerate", focusing rather on his "sick" and "despicable" spirit, for "the term Jew" denoted not just certain dominant "repulsive" physical traits, *"but rather"* -in Chamberlain's view- *"a special way of thinking and feeling"* (6). Rosenberg, the Nazi philosopher, hence asserted that the Jews *"are not properly a race, but an ancient racial mixture which has preserved its character by religious laws against intermarriage with other groups"* (7), exhibiting nonetheless dominant Semitic biological and moral features, admixed with a considerable amount of Negroid blood... Therefore, it was especially the Jew's spirit that the Nazis utterly despised as "decadent"; this explains Hitler's metaphysical hatred towards the "Jewish mind":

"Our racial pride is not aggressive except in so far as the Jewish race is concerned. We use the term Jewish race as a matter of convenience, for in reality and from the genetic point of view there is no such thing as the Jewish race... The Jewish race is first and foremost an abstract race of the mind... It is the characteristic mental makeup of his race which renders him impervious to the process of assimilation... And there in a nutshell is the proof of the superiority of the mind over the flesh" (8).

It was therefore the Jew's mental and spiritual makeup -much more than his biological inferiority- that made him such a "lower creature"; Nazism's "spiritual anti-Semitism" was thus even worse than the traditional religious anti-Semitism, for it considered that the Jew was both a biological *and* spiritual *Untermensch* (sub-human). It is ironic that William Bluhm should use the same passage mentioned above to conclude that Hitler viewed the Jews as a "counter-elite", as "competitors for the status of 'over-man' "!! Bluhm clearly and purposely misinterpreted Hitler's words, inverting what Hitler meant to say, and that is: that the Jew was first and foremost *spiritually* inferior to the Aryan, that he was a typical moral *Untermensch*, a "non-being", clearly not a competitor for the status of Superman! Hitler in fact agreed with Rosenberg's conception of Jews as an "anti-race",

"since their parasitic activity leads to the preservation of only those hereditary strains adapted to parasitism" (9).

Significantly, in addition to the undisputed influence of anti-Semitic philosophers like Chamberlain, Rosenberg, and others, on Nazi ideology, the anti-Semitism of the Nazis was also greatly inspired by Nietzsche's own fierce hostility to the Jews, a hostility that was in no way exaggerated by the Nazis. Thus did Nietzsche also warn against the dangers of the "Jewish soul" and the "Jewish instinct", which he perceived as profoundly vulgar (10), slavish, base, and decadent:

"People of the basest origin, in part rabble, outcasts not only from good but also from respectable society, raised away from even the smell of culture, without discipline, without knowledge, without the remotest suspicion that there is such a thing as conscience in spiritual matters; simply—Jews" (11).

In this virulently anti-Semitic passage, Nietzsche associates the word "Jew" with "base", "rabble", "outcast", "un-cultured", "un-disciplined", "ignorant", "unscrupulous"... The last two words "simply- Jews" have a considerable significance, since they clearly show how to Nietzsche, the radical aristocrat, the sole term "Jew" logically summarised everything he held in profound disdain. In another passage, Nietzsche deplores the "rabble-hotchpotch" of today in which the "Jew", i.e. the representative of "the rabble", is mixed up with the aristocratic gentleman:

"Ours is the kingdom of the rabble... Rabble, however, means hotchpotch. Rabble-Hotchpotch: in that everything is mixed up with everything else, saint and scoundrel and gentleman and Jew and every beast out of Noah's ark"(12).

To Nietzsche, we are living in the era of the "victory of the slave", best represented by the "decadent" Jew:

"Decay! Decay! Ne'er sank the world so low! Rome is now a harlot and a brothel too, Rome's Caesar a beast, and God himself- a Jew!" (13).

The climax of decay, Nietzsche thought, is that God himself is now a Jew: what could be more anti-Semitic?

Christianity, Democracy, and Marxism: products of the Jew, the "supreme decadent"

"Let us submit to the facts; that the people have triumphed- or the slaves, or the populace, or the herd, or whatever name you care to give them- if this happened through the Jews, so be it! In that case no nation ever had a greater mission in the world's history. The 'masters' have been done away with; the morality of the vulgar man has triumphed. This triumph may also be called a blood-poisoning (it has mutually fused the races)- I do not dispute it; but there is no doubt that this intoxication has succeeded. The 'redemption' of the human race (that is, from the masters) is progressing swimmingly; everything is obviously becoming Judaised, or Christianised, or vulgarised (what is there in the words?)"

Friedrich Nietzsche

"The Jewish doctrine of Marxism rejects the aristocratic principle of Nature and replaces the eternal privilege of power and strength by the mass of numbers and their dead weight. Thus it denies the value of personality in man, contests the significance of nationality and race, and thereby withdraws from humanity the premise of its existence and its culture. Through Marxism, the Jew tries to destroy, with every means, the racial foundations of the people he has set out to subjugate, pulling down the blood barriers between peoples...it was and it is Jews who bring the Negroes into the Rhineland, always with the same secret thought and clear aim of ruining the hated white race by the necessarily resulting bastardization, throwing it down from its cultural and political height, and himself rising to be its master... for a racially pure people which is conscious of its blood can never be enslaved by the Jew. In this world he will forever be master of bastards and bastards alone"

"Parliamentary democracy corresponds most closely to the Jew's requests because it eliminates the personality and in its place puts the majority of stupidity, incompetence, and last, but not least, cowardice"

Adolf Hitler

"Christianity, growing from Jewish roots and comprehensible only as a product of this soil, represents the reaction against that morality of breeding, of race, of privilege- it is the anti-Aryan religion par excellence: Christianity the revaluation of all Aryan values, the victory of Chandala values, the evangel preached to the poor and lowly, the collective rebellion

121

of everything downtrodden, wretched, ill-constituted, under-privileged against the 'race'- undying Chandala revenge as the religion of love…"

Friedrich Nietzsche

"Judaeo-Christianity, the greatest plague delivered by history"

Heinrich Himmler

"For the Indo-Aryan, religion is an inner experience drawn from the depths of the soul, independent of chronology and historical events, anti-rationalist and mystical, free from worship of images, strict retaliation, outward commandments, ritual formalism, and a privileged priest caste, its forms being pure and noble…

Jewish religiosity is characterised by selfishness, materialism, fanaticism, intolerance, narrowmindedness, formalism, precisianism, barren ritualism. The religion of the Jews is but the dread of a mighty idol holding out to its worshippers material enjoyments and the rule over other peoples as a recompense for submissiveness"

Houston Steward Chamberlain

"Paul, the Jew, the eternal Jew par excellence"

Friedrich Nietzsche

"Der Ewige Jude ("the eternal Jew")… an accursed specter, a carrier of deadly infection… The Jew's traits of character have remained the same, whether 2000 years ago as a grain dealer in Ostia, speaking Roman, or whether as a flour profiteer of today, jabbering German with a Jewish accent. It is always the same Jew"

Adolf Hitler

It was passages like the ones mentioned above -among many others- which prompted a Nietzsche scholar to assert that

"most of the stock of professional anti-Semitism is represented in Nietzsche: the Jews are intellectuals with a grievance, hence destroyers of what makes for stability in society; they run the press and the stock-exchange, to the disadvantage of the more honest and healthy Gentiles; they are parasites, decadents; they are responsible for the three great evils of modern civilization- Christianity, Democracy, Marxism" (14).

Indeed, Nietzsche believed that the egalitarian doctrines of Liberal Democracy and Marxism were but secularised versions of Christianity, a

Jewish religion which first invented the "myth" of the "equality of souls before God"... When Nietzsche says of the *"young stock exchange Jew"* that he is *"perhaps the most disgusting invention of mankind"* (15), there is every reason to believe that he is equating Jewry with Capitalism; and when he declares that the victory of Judea over Rome, in antiquity, was followed by yet another modern victory of Judea over the classical ideal *"in the French Revolution, and in a sense which was even more crucial and even more profound: the last political aristocracy that existed in Europe, that of the French seventeenth and eighteenth centuries, broke into pieces beneath the instincts of a resentful populace"* (16), Nietzsche is accusing the Jews of the worst crime against humanity: that of instigating the French Revolution, the "revolt of the slaves" which destroyed aristocracy -against which the Jews had the deepest hatred and grudge, for they, as "rabble", could never belong to it- a revolution which brought about the victory of the egalitarian doctrines of Democracy, Liberalism and Socialism, all of which are considered equally decadent by Nietzsche ...

The same charges against "world Jewry" were made a few decades later by the Nazis. Hitler indeed accused the Jews of being the instigators of the materialist and egalitarian doctrines of Marxism, Socialism, and Liberalism, which, the Fuehrer believed -as Nietzsche did- were based on Christianity's "Jewish idea" or "lie" of the equality of all men. The Jews aimed at establishing Democracy and the rule of parliamentarianism, for this system

"corresponds most closely to their requirements because it eliminates the personality -and in its place puts the majority of stupidity, incompetence, and last, but not least, cowardice" (17).

But the final aim of the Jews was -in Hitler's view- *"to replace the idea of democracy by the dictatorship of the proletariat"* (18), i.e. to impose the "Jewish doctrine of Marxism" which, by producing an artificial levelling of humanity under the slogan "equality of all men", is the sole hope of this Jewish "lower race" to end its historical enslavement by higher and stronger races, for this doctrine

"rejects the aristocratic principle of Nature and replaces the eternal privilege of power and strength by the mass of numbers and their dead weight. Thus it denies the value of personality in man, contests the significance of nationality and race, and thereby withdraws from humanity the premise of its existence and its culture" (19).

By shattering the personality and the race through the mixture and hence the contamination of races, Marxism removes the *"essential obstacle to the domination of the inferior being- and this is the Jew"* (20). Through Marxism, Hitler believed, the Jew thus *"tries to destroy, with every means, the racial foundations of the people he has set out to subjugate"*, pulling down the blood barriers between peoples. Indeed,

> *"it was and it is Jews who bring the Negroes into the Rhineland, always with the same secret thought and clear aim of ruining the hated white race by the necessarily resulting bastardization, throwing it down from its cultural and political height, and himself rising to be its master".*

For a racially pure people which is *"conscious of its blood"* can never be enslaved by that 'monstrous hybrid', the Jew:

> *"In this world he will forever be master over bastards and bastards alone"* *(21).*

By accusing the "subhuman" Jews of consciously striving to "intoxicate" and "bastardise" stronger and higher races as the only means to rule them, it was as though Hitler was quoting Nietzsche's following passage, in which he directs the same accusation of "blood-poisoning" against the Jews, condemning the latter for having succeeded in their "historical mission": achieving the victory of the "vulgar man" over the "masters", i.e. the "Judaisation" of the world:

> *"Let us submit to the facts; that the people have triumphed- or the slaves, or the populace, or the herd, or whatever name you care to give them- if this happened through the Jews, so be it! In that case no nation ever had a greater mission in the world's history. The 'masters' have been done away with; the morality of the vulgar man has triumphed. This triumph may also be called a blood-poisoning (it has mutually fused the races)- I do not dispute it; but there is no doubt that this intoxication has succeeded. The 'redemption' of the human race (that is, from the masters) is progressing swimmingly; everything is obviously becoming Judaised, or Christianised, or vulgarised (what is there in the words?)" (22).*

The last sentence clearly shows that Nietzsche -once again- equates the words "Jew" with "vulgar", stressing that these are just different words which nonetheless have the same essence and meaning ("what is there in the words?"). This passage leaves no doubt whatsoever as to Nietzsche's contempt for the Jews, *"a people 'born for slavery' as Tacitus and the whole ancient world says"* (23) - that world whose spirit Nietzsche took great pride in belonging to. Nietzsche indeed accuses the Jews, the "perfect slaves", of developing out of their resentment of their masters (Greeks, Romans, Egyptians, Assyrians, Babylonians, etc...) a "slave morality" represented by Judaeo-Christianity, Democracy, Liberalism, Socialism, all of which were "decadent" movements mainly instigated by Jewry. Christianity, a typical incarnation of this slavish morality, was -in Nietzsche's view- mainly the product of the Jews, the logical and "ultimate Jewish consequence", and not -as Christian anti-Semites like to believe- a counter-movement against the Jewish instinct. In this context, Walter Kaufmann's argument that, because Nietzsche hated Christians and Jews alike, his anti-Christianity was therefore not motivated by anti-Semitism, can easily be refuted by the simple fact that Nietzsche hated Christians *precisely* because he perceived them as "nothing but Jews":

*"The Christian is only a Jew of a 'freer confession'" (24)... the Christian...
is the Jew once more- even thrice more" (25).*

Nietzsche repudiated Christianity -or what he liked to call "Judaised Christianity"- precisely *because* of its Jewish origins! Indeed, in the *Antichrist*, one of Nietzsche's major works, a primarily anti-Semitic book which clearly reveals his racial -and racist- views, Nietzsche says of Christianity that it is the "anti-Aryan religion *par excellence*":

*"Christianity, growing from Jewish roots and comprehensible only as
a product of this soil, represents the reaction against that morality of
breeding, of race, of privilege-it is the anti-Aryan religion par excellence:
Christianity the revaluation of all Aryan values, the victory of Chandala
values, the evangel preached to the poor and lowly, the collective rebellion
of everything downtrodden, wretched, ill-constituted, under-privileged
against the 'race'-undying Chandala revenge as the religion of love..."
(26).*

Judaeo-Christian values, or "Chandala values" (the Chandala are the "outcasts", the "untouchables" who were considered as a lower species and thus excluded from the Indo-European racial caste system) versus Aryan values: that was -according to Nietzsche- the spiritual conflict characterising world history. The Jews used Christianity to "Judaise" the whole world with their Chandala values, and they were therefore guilty of the worst crime, that of revaluating all aristocratic values, i.e. Aryan pagan values. Nietzsche believed that the Judaisation of Christianity itself (i.e. the distortion and the most incredible inversion of the Gospel, of Christ's original message, or what Nietzsche favourably calls "primitive

Christianity"), and the subsequent gradual Judaisation of the world through Christianity, was mainly the work of Paul *"the Jew, the eternal Jew par excellence"*, Paul, *"Chandala hatred against Rome, against 'the world', become flesh and genius"* (27). Indeed, Paul, according to Nietzsche, embodied

> *"the antithetical type to the 'bringer of glad tidings', the genius of hatred, of the vision of hatred, of the inexorable logic of hatred... The redeemer above all: he nailed him to his Cross. The life, the example, the teaching, the death, the meaning and the right of the entire Gospel"* (28).

Paul, the "eternal Jew", *"annulled primitive Christianity as a matter or principle"*. That, for Nietzsche, was the tragic irony of history: Paul

> *"re-erected on a grand scale precisely that which Christ had annulled through his way of living... The church is precisely that against which Jesus preached- and against which he taught his disciples to fight"* (29).

Judaeo-Christianity, the perfect incarnation of the Jewish spirit represented by Paul, was therefore the exact opposite of primitive, non-Jewish Christianity; thus did Nietzsche affirm: *"Deus, qualem Paulus creavit, dei negatio"* ("God, as Paul created him, is a denial of God") (30). The Jews had even distorted God's image *("God himself- a Jew!")*... This explains the deep sense of Nietzsche's "godlessness", for Nietzsche thought that it was precisely his belief in the *true* God which had pushed him to deny the Jewish God of Christianity.

It is worth noting here that the typically anti-Semitic term *Der Ewige Jude* -"the Eternal Jew"- used by Nietzsche to describe Paul, has a particular significance, since it was also a favourite expression in Nazi racist propaganda designating the Jew's parasitic life which allows him to survive at the expense of other peoples: *"Der Ewige Jude... an accursed specter, a figure who can neither live nor die and remains an amalgam of murderer, corpse, and survivor remnant. He is death-tainted but survives everyone* (the Wandering Jew was described as having 'buried the Egyptians, the Greeks, and the Romans') *and therefore represents the ultimate embodiment of survivor contagion, of a carrier of deadly infection"* (31). The Jew is eternal, in Hitler's view, because his sneaky deceitful tactics remain the same, and enable him to survive more honest and nobler races... The Jew's traits of character have therefore

> *"remained the same, whether two thousand years ago as a grain dealer in Ostia, speaking Roman, or whether as a flour profiteer of today, jabbering German with a Jewish accent. It is always the same Jew"* (32).

The Nazis -like Nietzsche- accused the Jews of corrupting and distorting Christ's original message -which mainly consisted of the purely Aryan pagan concept of the "inner Christ" or "Son of God", i.e. the God-Man, and the possibility of human perfection- into its very opposite, namely Judaeo-Christianity, with its Semitic notion of a transcendental God forever unreachable to his sinful, imperfect "servants"; the Jews were thus charged with turning Christianity from an Aryan religion preaching the God-Man into a Semitic egalitarian doctrine which preaches the equality of all men, submissiveness, meekness, pity, and humility, as well as the impossibility of human perfection due to man's sinful, lower nature... Indeed, H.S. Chamberlain, one of the spiritual godfathers of the Third Reich, who considered that the conception of sin, of a Hell and a Devil was *a Jewish invention*" (33), contrasted the Aryan with the Semitic view of religion: whereas for the Indo-Aryan, religion was *"an inner experience drawn from the depths of the soul, independent of chronology and historical events, anti-rationalist and mystical, free from worship of images, strict retaliation, outward commandments, ritual formalism, and a privileged priest caste, its forms being pure and noble"*, Jewish religiosity was characterised by *"selfishness, materialism, fanaticism, intolerance, narrowmindedness, formalism, precisianism, barren ritualism"*. The religion of the Jews, according to Chamberlain, is

"but the dread of a mighty idol holding out to its worshippers material enjoyments and the rule over other peoples as a recompense for submissiveness" (34).

The Aryan genius is immanentist, an elevation from Man to God; the Semitic spirit -best exemplified by the Jew- is transcendentalist, a fall from God to Man...

The Jew, a typical incarnation of Slave Morality

"The Jewish people handled the pia fraus ("pious fraud", or "holy lie") with such perfection, such a degree of 'good conscience', that one cannot be sufficiently cautious when it preaches morality. When Jews step forward as innocence itself then the danger is great"

Friedrich Nietzsche

"Existence impels the Jew to lie, and to lie perpetually... the Jew, the great master in lying"

Adolf Hitler

"The Jews are the counterparts of decadents: they have known how to place themselves at the head of all decadent movements (-as the Christianity of Paul) so as to make of them something stronger than any party affirmative of life... the final aim of the Jew, his life-interest, is to make mankind sick... Jewish hate, that most profound and sublime hate, the hatred of weakness... with the Jews begins the slave revolt in morals"

Friedrich Nietzsche

"The Jew is a culture destroyer, for he lacks those qualities which distinguish the races that are creative and hence culturally blessed... the Jew possesses no culture-creating force of any sort, since the idealism, without which there is no true higher development of man, is not present in him and never was present"

Adolf Hitler

"The Jews, a people born for slavery... It was, in fact, with the Jews that the revolt of the slaves begins in the sphere of morals... The symbol of the (master-slave) fight... is called 'Rome against Judea, Judea against Rome'... The Romans were the strong and aristocratic; a nation stronger and more aristocratic has never existed in the world, has never been dreamed of... The Jews, conversely, were that priestly nation of resentment par excellence, possessed by a unique genius for popular morals... It is at least certain that sub hoc signo Israel, with its revenge and transvaluation of all values, has up to the present always triumphed again over all other ideals, over all more aristocratic ideals... all that has been done on earth against 'the noble', 'the powerful', 'the masters', 'the rulers', fades into nothing compared with what the Jews have done against them"

Friedrich Nietzsche

"The Aryan-Semitic conflict: Rome against Judea" Alfred Rosenberg

"The Jews are far removed from us as animals are from humans... I do not mean that I look upon Jews as animals; they are much further removed from animals as we are... Therefore, it is not a crime against humanity to exterminate them since they do not belong to humanity. They are creatures outside nature"

"Eternal nature inexorably avenges the infringement of her commands. Hence today I believe that I am acting in accordance with the will of the Almighty creator: by defending myself against the Jew, I am fighting for the work of the Lord"

Adolf Hitler

In addition to the charges of instigating decadent movements like Judaeo-Christianity, Liberalism and Socialism, thus corrupting politics *and* religion, Nietzsche and the Nazis also held the Jews responsible for producing out of their vengefulness and resentment against the world a "slave revolt in morals", undertaking the most incredible and most thorough falsification of history and morality, and rendering everything as unnatural and fake as possible through a complete inversion of all noble and aristocratic values... Hitler, who declared that *"existence impels the Jew to lie, and to lie perpetually"*, delightfully adopting Schopenhauer's depiction of the Jew as *"the great master in lying"* (35), was clearly inspired by Nietzsche when the latter said of the Jewish people that it

"handled the pia fraus ("pious fraud", or "holy lie") with such perfection, such a degree of 'good conscience', that one cannot be sufficiently cautious when it preaches morality. When Jews step forward as innocence itself then the danger is great" (36).

The Jews, according to Nietzsche, distorted all nature, all reality, transformed themselves into a living antithesis to natural conditions... They turned virtually all history, religion, culture, philosophy, morals upside down; the Jewish mind

"resolved all reality (history, nature) into a holy un-naturalness and unreality- which no longer recognized real history, which was no longer interested in natural consequences" (37).

This falsehood was also denounced by Hitler, who accused the Jew of trampling on history, tradition, ethics, morality, and everything great in the world:

"In the political field he refuses the state the means for its self-preservation, destroys the foundations of all national self-maintenance and defence, destroys faith in the leadership, scoffs at its history and past, and drags everything that is truly great into the gutter. Culturally he contaminates art, literature, the theatre, makes a mockery of natural feeling, overthrows all concepts of beauty and sublimity, of the noble and the good, and instead drags men down into the sphere of his own base nature. Religion is ridiculed, ethics and morality represented as outmoded, until the last drops of a nation in its struggle for existence in this world have fallen" (38).

In the above passage, Hitler fully embraces Nietzsche's description of the Jews as the "radical falsifiers" of *"all nature, all naturalness, all reality, the entire inner world as well as the outer*", defining themselves "*counter to all those conditions under which a nation was previously able to live, was permitted to live*". The Jews, in Nietzsche's view, made of themselves

"*an antithesis to natural conditions- they inverted religion, religious worship, morality, history, psychology one after the other in an irreparable way into the contradiction of their natural values*" (39).

The Jews, the anti-natural people *par excellence*, distort everything they come across, for they "*have no true culture on their own*", as Hitler says, and thus the "*sham culture*" they today possess "*is the property of other peoples, and for the most part, is ruined in their hands.* Indeed, Hitler asserts, "*there has never been an original Jewish art, architecture and music*", and what the Jews do accomplish in these fields is "*either patchwork or intellectual theft*". Thus, the Jew is a "culture-destroyer", for he

"*lacks those qualities which distinguish the races that are creative and hence culturally blessed... The Jew possesses no culture-creating force of any sort, since the idealism, without which there is no true higher development of man, is not present in him and never was present*" (40).

The Nazis therefore totally agreed with Nietzsche's description of the Jews as the supreme decadents, a nation whose "resentment morality" led it to take the side of all

"*decadence instincts... The Jews are the counterpart of decadents: they have known how to place themselves at the head of all decadence movements (-as the Christianity of Paul) so as to make of them something stronger than any party affirmative of life*" (41).

But decadence was only a means: the final aim of the Jew, his life-interest, Nietzsche believed, was to

"*make mankind sick*" and "*invert the concepts 'good' and 'evil', 'true' and 'false' in a mortally dangerous and world-calumniating sense. The history of Israel is invaluable as a typical history of the denaturalizing of natural values*" (42).

Jewish hate, "*that most profound and sublime hate, which creates ideals and changes old values to new creations, the like of which has never been on earth*" (43), this "hatred of weakness" led the Jews to accomplish the greatest inversion of values in history, starting a "slave revolt in morals", as shown in Nietzsche's following passages:

"The Jews achieved that miracle of inversion of values thanks to which life on earth has for a couple of millennia acquired a new and dangerous fascination- their prophets fused 'rich', 'godless', 'evil', 'violent', 'sensual' into one and were the first to coin the word 'world' as a word of infamy. It is in this inversion of values (with which is involved the employment of the word for 'poor' as a synonym of 'holy' and 'friend') that the significance of the Jewish people resides: with them begins the slave revolt in morals" (44).

This radical inversion of values aimed at replacing the "Master Morality" of the aristocratic Roman rulers by its exact antithesis, the "Slave Morality" of the subjected Jewish "rabble":

"The Jews, that priestly nation which eventually realised that the one method of effecting satisfaction on its enemies and tyrants was by means of a radical transvaluation of values, which was at the same time an act of the cleverest revenge... It was the Jews who, in opposition to the aristocratic equation (Good = aristocratic = beautiful = happy = loved by the gods), dared with a terrifying logic to suggest the contrary equation, and indeed to maintain with the teeth of the most profound hatred (the hatred of weakness) this contrary equation, namely, 'the wretched are the alone the good; the poor, the weak, the lowly, are alone the good; the suffering, the needy, the sick, the loathsome, are the only ones who are pious, the only ones who are blessed, for them alone is salvation- but you, on the other hand, you aristocrats, you men of power, you are to all eternity the evil, the horrible, the covetous, the insatiate, the godless; eternally also shall you be unblessed, the cursed, the damned!' We know who it was who reaped the heritage of this Jewish transvaluation... it was, in fact, with the Jews that the revolt of the slaves begins in the sphere of morals; that revolt which has behind it a history of two millennia, and which at the present day has only moved out of our sight, because it- has achieved victory" (45).

Thus, according to the Nietzschean and Nazi doctrines, the Master-Slave conflict was best represented by the struggle between Rome and Judea, respectively incarnating the Aryan aristocratic spirit and the Jewish slavish spirit, a conflict which Nietzsche described as follows:

"The symbol of this fight... throughout the course of history up to the present time, is called 'Rome against Judea, Judea against Rome'. Hitherto there has been no greater event than that fight, the putting of that question, that deadly antagonism. Rome found in the Jew the incarnation of the

unnatural, as though it were its diametrically opposed monstrosity, and in Rome the Jew was held to be convicted of hatred of the whole human race: and rightly so, in so far as it is right to link the well-being and the future of the human race to the unconditional mastery of the aristocratic values, of the Roman values... The Romans were the strong and aristocratic; a nation stronger and more aristocratic has never existed in the world, has never been dreamed of... The Jews, conversely, were that priestly nation of resentment par excellence, possessed by a unique genius for popular morals: just compare with the Jews the nations with analogous gifts, such as the Chinese or the Germans, so as to realise afterwards what is first rate, and what is fifth rate" (46).

Nietzsche believed that Judea's vengeful distortion and revaluation of all nobler values, stemming from an indelibly slavish trait in the Jewish character, had undoubtedly guaranteed, through Christianity, its triumph against Rome:

"Which one of them has been provisionally victorious, Rome or Judea? but there is not a shadow of a doubt; just consider to whom in Rome itself you nowadays bow down, as though before the quintessence of all the highest values- and not only in Rome, but almost in over half the world, everywhere where man has been tamed or is about to be tamed- to three Jews, as we know, and one Jewess (to Jesus of Nazareth, to Peter the fisher, to Paul the tent-maker, and to the mother of the aforesaid Jesus, named Mary). This is very remarkable: Rome is undoubtedly defeated.... Rome herself... the new Judaised Rome" (47)... It is at least certain that sub hoc signo Israel, with its revenge and transvaluation of all values, has up to the present always triumphed again over all other ideals, over all more aristocratic ideals" (48).

Nietzsche could not be more emphatic in his depiction of the Jews as the typical resentful slaves:

"All that has been done on earth against 'the noble', 'the powerful', 'the masters', 'the rulers', fades into nothing compared with what the Jews have done against them" (49).

At this point it would be idle to even conceive of questioning Nietzsche's virulent anti-Semitism. In fact, Nietzsche was as vehement as the most fanatical Nazis in his condemnation of the Jew, which both doctrines considered alien to the natural order. This explains Hitler's metaphysical contempt for the Jews, whom he viewed as "racial degenerates", as "sub-humans" far removed from mankind, even lower than the animal: *"they are as far removed from us as animals are from humans"*, said Hitler, carefully explaining: *"I do not mean that I look upon Jews as animals; they are much further removed from animals than we are"*. Therefore, it is not a crime against humanity to exterminate them *"since they do not belong to humanity. They are creatures outside nature"* (50). It was thus a sacred duty to "eliminate" these "fake men", these "non-beings" who represent the living antithesis to divine Nature:

> *"Eternal Nature inexorably avenges the infringement of her commands. Hence today I believe that I am acting in accordance with the will of the Almighty creator: by defending myself against the Jew, I am fighting for the work of the Lord"* (51).

One wonders how, given the above statements, Bluhm could still persist in his ludicrous assumption that Hitler perceived the Jews as the Nazis' "competitors for the status of 'over-man' "!!! All the evidence and the facts point to the following certainty: Nietzsche's Anti-Semitism was in no way less virulent than Nazi Anti-Semitism: indeed, both Nietzsche and the Nazis held the Jew in utter contempt, despising him as the typical *Untermensch*, the supreme decadent who incarnates the slave morality in all its manifestations... Both doctrines viewed the Jew as a resentful and deceitful "lower species" of man, accusing him of placing himself at the head of all "decadent" movements, namely Judaeo-Christianity, the French Revolution, Democracy, Liberalism, Socialism,... thereby corrupting mankind and hampering its progress through a thorough and unprecedented act of falsification of history and morality, and through an inversion of all noble values caused by a "slave revolt in morals"... The Jew had waged an all-out war against everything that is noble and natural, against tradition, the value of the race, the morality of breeding, privilege, the order of rank... He is therefore the perfect antithesis to the Superman...

CHAPTER SIX

NIETZSCHE: THE PROPHET OF NAZISM

"And when we call out to this youth, marching under the Swastika: 'Heil Hitler!' at the same time we greet with the call Friedrich Nietzsche!"

Alfred Bauemler

Nazi Nietzschean scholar

The main objective -indeed, the very significance- of the present book lies in its endeavour to prove that Nietzsche was the prophet of Nazism, thus putting an end to the controversy that still divides scholars over the Nietzsche-Nazi connection. It is my opinion that this objective has been reached, for the extensive, in-depth analysis of both the Nietzschean and Nazi doctrines undertaken throughout this work has revealed Nietzsche's tremendous influence on Nazi ideology, highlighting the striking similarities between the two doctrines, and showing how Nietzsche's major assumptions were fully adopted by the Nazis, becoming an integral -and characteristic- part of Nazi ideology.

Indeed, both Nietzsche and the Nazis were vehement neo-pagans calling for a revival of pre-Christian Aryan paganism, the "Natural Religion" mainly based on ancient Aryan mythology and the "esoteric tradition" from India to Greece (Manu, the Vedas, Brahmanism, Zarathustra, Dionysus, Prometheus, ...). Thus, "Esoteric Nazism", or the Nazi cult, was a modern occult phenomenon, a spiritual movement with a new vision of the universe heralding the advent of a New Age for mankind, and preaching the coming of a race of god-men or Supermen (as exemplified by Nazism's main symbols, the Swastika and the double S rune), and was thereby a truly Nietzschean movement. As staunch neo-pagans, Nietzsche and the Nazis considered themselves as heirs to the Hyperboreans or Atlanteans, the original legendary Aryans, and viewed the ancient Greek world as the pagan ideal embodying the aristocratic spirit at its best, thus venerating a veritable "cult of antiquity". Also, both doctrines believed in the "Eternal Recurrence", the ancient Aryanist theory of evolutionary cycles. Furthermore, both Nietzsche and the Nazis rejected Semitic Judaeo-Christianity, considering it a Jewish religion for the sick and the weak, a gross distortion of the original teachings of Christ, whom they admired as a spiritual liberator, and whose message, which focused on the Aryan concept of the "Inner Christ" or God-Man, they fully embraced; thus they contrasted Christ the hero, the Aryan rebel against the "Jewish spirit", with transcendental Judaeo-Christianity, the "anti-Aryan religion".

A central theme in Nietzsche's philosophy is the Will to Power concept, which the Nazis wholly embraced; thus did Nietzsche and the Nazis acknowledge the Will to Power as the motor of history, the life principle and ultimate reality. Indeed, Nazism embraced Nietzsche's definition of the Will to Power as the origin of morality (itself being a morality of Masters "beyond good and evil"), as well as Nietzsche's famous proclamation of the "death" of the "transcendent God" of Judaeo-Christianity, i.e. the self-overcoming of Christian morality and its conception of "another world" as a flight from -and a curse to- the present world; the "death of God" thus meant Man's great liberation and his possibility to become divine and thus to achieve perfection in the here and now. The "active nihilism" or "spiritual atheism" advanced by Nietzsche and espoused by Nazism was thus the immanentist alternative to the transcendentalism of the Western Judaeo-Christian tradition, postulating the Will to Power as the sole truth, the only reachable goal on earth. The Nazis also adopted Nietzsche's division of the world between the natural-born "Masters" and the natural-born "slaves", or the "minority" versus the "majority", each having their own distinct morality, and –in line with Nietzschean thought- Nazism admitted that the "Slave Morality" was actually predominant due to the victory of the egalitarian "slavish" doctrines of Christianity, Socialism and Liberalism, the fact which required a radical transvaluation of values in order to impose, in the modern world, the "Master Morality" which was prevalent in pagan antiquity; hence the "immoralism" preached by both doctrines...

Yet Nietzsche and the Nazis were no nihilists; their "active nihilism" is but a means to destroy the corrupt "old law-tables" and to replace them by new aristocratic values that would give a real meaning to the world following the "twilight of the idols", i.e. the superstitions that have hitherto kept man in chains, hampering his progress. The concept of the Will to Power thus acquires a new dimension and a creative meaning: self-overcoming and the Superman, i.e. the man who has overcome himself... Indeed, both Nietzsche and the Nazis preached self-overcoming as life's highest goal, ultimately leading to the *Uebermensch* ("Superman"), the perfect man in body and soul who would fill the vacant divine throne after the proclamation of the death of the transcendent God (i.e., man was now free to become divine). Contrasting the Will to Power as creative self-overcoming with the mere will to self-preservation of the 'vegetating' Liberals and Socialists, the Nietzschean and Nazi doctrines stressed on the Higher Man's willingness and ability to sacrifice himself for the sake of the sacred mission of breeding a higher humanity. The Superman hence refuses to kneel before a "god in heaven", venerating instead the "god within" and thus becomes a God-Man, realising perfection in this world instead of waiting for a promise of eternal bliss in the "other" world...

Another dimension of Nietzsche's concept of the Will to Power, which the Nazis fully adopted, is the drive for conquest and domination.

Indeed, both the Nietzschean and Nazi doctrines glorified war as higher life affirmation, as the natural state, the "great purifier"; yet the war they venerated was not an aimless urge for violence and destruction, it was rather a "holy war" in the service of producing a higher humanity, a war waged by "political" or "ideological" warriors quite similar to Plato's class of "Guardians". Nietzsche in fact contrasted his "warriors" -the "fighters for Knowledge"- with mere "soldiers". Nietzsche and the Nazis considered it a right and a duty of the strong minority, the natural aristocrats, the creators, to dominate and oppress the weak majority, the "many-too-many", the shapeless, useless, vegetating "herd", in compliance with the law of natural selection, asserting that exploitation, cruelty, slavery, and even the annihilation of "millions of human failures" as a "breeding process" (in Nietzsche's exact words!) have always been a characteristic feature of -and are therefore of the very essence of- all great cultures and true progress.

The aristocratic worldview of the Nietzschean and Nazi philosophies, whose highest aim was to breed a universal Master Race that would rule the earth, thus led them to despise all "enemies of the Superman", namely the egalitarian doctrines of Liberalism and Socialism, or what Nietzsche termed the rule of the "Last Man", of modernity's "Men without chests". The radically aristocratic Nietzschean and Nazi perfectionist doctrines in fact had but utter contempt for Western Civilisation (based on the Judaeo-Christian tradition, 19th century Enlightenment, and Rationalism) and its two products, Liberal parliamentarian Democracy and Socialism, considering that these ideologies represented "mob rule", the victory of the slave, and that their levelling character and highest aim, the will to mere self-preservation, could never produce greatness, could never offer the alternative to -but only perpetuate- the nihilism caused by the "death of God", producing instead a "cult of the mediocre" in all things. This "aristocratic radicalism" which Nietzsche and Nazism embraced, represented a "third option" between the two "corrupt" doctrines of Socialism and Liberalism- primarily aimed at consciously breeding a New Aristocracy of blood and spirit (eliminating in the process all "life unworthy of life"), a nobility which -much like Plato's Republic- would be recruited from all social classes.

According to Nietzsche and Nazism, that new nobility destined to rule the earth was none other than the "Aryan and conquering Master Race", a universal race of Supermen transcending the political boundaries of states and nations. Indeed, both the Nietzschean and Nazi doctrines were universal -yet radically elitist- in character, despising "narrow politics", i.e. the liberal "minimal state", whose sole end was the protection of "Life, Liberty, and Property", in favour of a supra-national "spiritual racism", or what Nietzsche termed "Great Politics": a strong, highly authoritarian and hierarchical supra-national state which would act as a means for a higher goal, that of breeding the Master Race, and would therefore be the blueprint for an Aristocratic World Government; such was Nietzsche's vision of the future Europe, and Nazism's "supra-national Aryan State" or "Germanic Europe". Nietzsche and Hitler considered that the Germans - despite their conversion to Christianity (which weakened and corrupted them) and their "racial degradation" through inter-mixture with "lower races"- had an essential role to play in the "Great Politics" of the future, for they still were more manly and more creative than most peoples on the surface of the globe. Thus did the Nazis come up with a unique ideology, "racist nationalism", in an attempt to reconcile the often conflicting doctrines of racism and nationalism, turning Nazi Germany into the racial and spiritual centre for all the Aryans of the world, a nation from which would spring the future "Lords of the earth".

Finally, a characteristic feature of both the Nietzschean and Nazi doctrines is their virulent anti-Semitism, a racist-aristocratic and spiritual anti-Semitism which -unlike the traditional Christian anti-Semitism targeting the Jews as a religious community- condemned the "Jewish spirit", accusing the Jew of being the supreme decadent, the typical *Untermensch,* the instigator and living incarnation of the slave morality in all its manifestations (Judaeo-Christianity, Socialism, Liberalism, Democracy...). According to Nietzsche and the Nazis, it was the Jew, that "great master in lying", who produced a radical distortion and falsification of history and a total inversion of the pagan aristocratic values; it was the same "eternal Jew", the slave who, out of his resentment and vengefulness against his masters (Greeks, Romans, ...) brought about the "slave revolt in morals" which is prevailing today, gradually "Judaising" -i.e. corrupting- the world through the Christian values of submissiveness, meekness, pity, humility. And it is still the Jew who is using the Christian "holy lie" of the "equality of souls before God" -a lie which was embraced by Liberalism and Marxism, secularised versions of Christianity- to produce a bastardisation or "blood poisoning" of the world as the only means for this "lower creature" to rule over strong, healthy and creative races. Nietzsche and the Nazis thus dismissed the Jew from civilisation and culture, considering him alien to the natural order, the living antithesis to the Aryan Superman.

The Nazis were pagans; they despised Judaeo-Christianity as the "anti-Aryan religion *par excellence*"; they believed that the Will to Power is the law of life; their highest goal was the creation of the Superman; they venerated war as higher life-affirmation; they regarded the exploitation or annihilation of "lower races" as a natural -even a necessary- characteristic of Culture; they held a radically aristocratic view of the world, dividing men into "Masters" and "Slaves"; they despised the egalitarian doctrines of Liberalism and Socialism; they advocated the conscious and organised breeding of a universal Master Race, viewing the state as nothing but a means to the attainment of that goal; they had but utter contempt for the Jew, that "typical slave" behind the "decadent" movements of Judaeo-Christianity, Liberalism, and Socialism... All of these values and ideals so characteristic of Nazism were also the main tenets of the Nietzschean philosophy, the fact which brings us to the following conclusion, despite all attempts by some scholars to distort and falsify this certainty: The Nazis were indisputably true Nietzscheans, and Nietzsche was their prophet. Indeed, with the advent of Nazism, it was as though Zarathustra had gone back to the valley to teach humanity -once again- the Superman, making sure this time to actually impose the rule of the Superman by the force of arms...

When the endless columns of steel-helmeted SS "Supermen" marched beneath the Swastika at the massive martial displays and pagan ceremonies of the 1930s, Germany was effectively hailing the Nazi One Thousand Year Reich, or Nietzsche's self-proclaimed *"great, far-off empire of man, the thousand-year empire of Zarathustra"* (1). Nazism was primarily an ideology that was loyally dedicated to the creation and the rule of Nietzsche's Superman; it was as though the Nazis had only to put Nietzsche's words into motion. In fact, Hitler's *"Mein Kampf... could hardly have been written without the aid of two of the great names in the cultural heritage of the world: Richard Wagner and Friedrich Nietzsche"* (2). And thus, Nietzsche's Zarathustra became the bible of the Nazis, who proclaimed themselves his holy warriors, as Alfred Bauemler, the Nazi official interpreter of Nietzsche, overtly declared:

> *"And when we call out to this youth, marching under the swastika: 'Heil Hitler!' at the same time we greet with the call Friedrich Nietzsche!"* (3).

However, despite the striking similarities between Nietzsche's philosophy and the Secret Nazi doctrine, one still has to wonder whether any model, ideology or system could fully express the greatness and depth of Nietzsche's soul, or embody his overflowing spirit. All attempts - from both the Left and the Right - to appropriate Nietzsche's philosophy and distort its universal and eternal essence and scope are doomed to fail, for his unique thought of a higher order remains an infinite source of inspiration, an eternal call to create -evermore- the Superman, who, like Dionysus, will be "eternally reborn and return again from destruction".

ENDNOTES

INTRODUCTION

1. H.F. Peters quoted in Bruce Detwiler, *Nietzsche and the Politics of Aristocratic Radicalism* (Chicago and London: The University of Chicago Press, 1990), p.2.

CHAPTER ONE

1. Bruce Detwiler, *ibid*, p.5.

CHAPTER TWO

1. *"The Romans were the strong and aristocratic; a nation stronger and more aristocratic has never existed in the world, has never been dreamed of"*. Friedrich Nietzsche, *On the Genealogy of Morals* (New York: Russel & Russel Inc., 1964), p. 54-55.

2. Bruce Detwiler, *Nietzsche and the Politics of Aristocratic Radicalism* (Chicago and London: The University of Chicago Press, 1990), p.190.

3. Friedrich Nietzsche, *The Will to Power* (New York: Random House, 1967), p.503.

4. Friedrich Nietzsche, *Twilight of the Idols* (London: Penguin Books, 1990), p.119.

5. Friedrich Nietzsche, *The Will to Power, op. cit.*, p.533.

6. J.S. Conway, *The Nazi Persecution of the Churches 1933–45* (New York: Basic Books, Inc., 1968), p.141.

7. Gerald Suster, *Hitler Black Magician* (London: Skoob Books Ltd, 1996), p.40.

8. *ibid*, p.49.

9. *ibid*, p.49.

10. *ibid*, pp.105, 159.

11. *ibid*,p. 48.

12. Louis Pauwels & Jacques Bergier, *The Morning of the Magicians* (New York: Stein and Day, 1963), p.151.

13. Nicholas Goodrick-Clarcke, *The Occult Roots of Nazism- Secret Aryan Cults and their Influence on Nazi Ideology* (London, New York: I.B. Tauris & Co. Ltd., 1992), p.218.

14. Pauwels & Bergier, *op. cit.*, p.203.

15. Michael Howard, *The Occult Conspiracy- Secret Societies: Their Influence and Power in World History* (Rochester, Vermont: Destiny Books, 1989), p.131.

16. Gerald Suster, *op. cit.*, p.178.

17. *ibid*, p.180.

18. James M. Peterson, *The Enchanted Alphabet- A Guide to Authentic Rune Magic and Divination* (England: The Aquarian Press, 1988), p.120.

19. Friedrich Nietzsche, *The Antichrist* (London: Penguin Books, 1990), p.191.

20. Friedrich Nietzsche, *The Birth of Tragedy* (New York: Russel & Russel Inc., 1964), p.157.

21. Friedrich Nietzsche, *The Antichrist, op. cit.*, p.127.

22. Nicholas Goodrick-Clarcke, *op. cit.*, p.220.

23. Gerald Suster, *op. cit.*, p.101. Also, according to Madame Helena Petrovna Blavatsky, the founder of the Theosophical Society which greatly influenced Nazi thought, the second hyperborean "root-race" had dwelt on "a vanished polar continent"...

24. Friedrich Nietzsche, *The Will to Power, op. cit.*, p.225.

25. Richard Noll, *The Jung Cult- Origins of a Charismatic Movement* (New Jersey: Princeton University Press, 1994), p.86.

26. Friedrich Nietzsche, *The Birth of Tragedy*, op. cit., pp.76, 77, 78, 79.

27. Adolf Hitler, *Mein Kampf* (Boston: Houghton Mifflin Company, 1971), p.290.

28. Helena Petrovna Blavatsky, *The Secret Doctrine* (Los Angeles: The Theosophical Company, 1982), pp.413-14.

29. Nicholas Goodrick-Clarcke, *op. cit.*, p.52.

30. J.S. Conway, *op. cit.*, p.153.

31. Adolf Hitler, *op. cit.*, p. 497.

32. Carl Gustav Jung, *Nietzsche's Zarathustra* (New Jersey: Princeton University Press, 1988), p.377.

33. Pauwels & Bergier, *op. cit.*, p.196.

34. *ibid*, p. 197.

35. Gerald Suster, *op. cit.*, p.125.

36. Helena P. Blavatsky, *op. cit.*, pp.99, 100.

37. Friedrich Nietzsche, *Thus Spoke Zarathustra* (London: Penguin Books, 1969), p.234.

38. Crane Brinton, *Nietzsche* (Cambridge, Massachusetts: Harvard University Press, 1941), p.140.

39. Nicholas Goodrick-Clarcke, *op. cit.*, p.20.

40. Helena P. Blavatsky, *op. cit.*, p.99.

41. Friedrich Nietzsche, *The Will to Power,* *op. cit.,* pp.542-3.

42. Albert Chandler, *Rosenberg's Nazi Myth* (New York: Greenwood Press, 1968), p.43.

43. Friedrich Nietzsche, *The Antichrist,* *op. cit.,* p.195.

44. George Allen Morgan, *What Nietzsche Means* (New York: Harper Torchbooks, 1944), p.346.

45. Friedrich Nietzsche, *The Will to Power,* *op. cit.,* pp.114-5.

46. Crane Brinton, *op. cit.,* pp.102-3).

47. Herbert Ziegler, *Nazi Germany's New Aristocracy- The SS Leadership, 1925-1939* (New Jersey: Princeton University Press, 1989), p.90.

48. Friedrich Nietzsche, *The Antichrist,* *op. cit.,* p.129.

49. Friedrich Nietzsche, *The Will to Power,* *op. cit.,* p.101.

50. Friedrich Nietzsche, *The Antichrist,* *op. cit.,* p.160.

51. Herbert Ziegler, *op. cit.,* p.85.

52. J.S. Conway, *op. cit.,* p.330.

53. Gerald Suster, *op. cit.,* p.112.

54. Crane Brinton,; *op. cit.,* p.223-4.

55. Carl Gustav Jung, *The Psychology of Nazism* (New Jersey: Princeton University Press, 1989), p.11.

56. George L. Mosse, *Nazi Culture- Intellectual, Cultural and Social Life in the Third Reich* (New York: Grosset & Dunlap, 1966), p.256.

57. Walter Kaufmann, *Nietzsche: Philosopher, Psychologist, Antichrist* (New Jersey: Princeton University Press, 1974), p.297.

58. *ibid,* p.290.

59. Friedrich Nietzsche, *The Antichrist, op. cit.*, p.156.

60. Houston Stewart Chamberlain, *Foundations of the Nineteenth Century* (London: John Lane The Bodley Head, 1912), p.5.

61. *ibid*, p.193.

62. Frank H. Hankins, *The Racial Basis of Civilization- A Critique of the Nordic Doctrine* (New York & London: Alfred .A. Knopf, 1926), p.86.

63. Alber Chandler, *op. cit.*, p.43.

64. H.S. Chamberlain, op. cit., p.193.

65. *ibid*, 199.

66. Adolf Hitler, *op. cit.*, p.307.

67. George L. Mosse, *op. cit.*, p.104.

68. Nicholas Goodrick-Clarcke, *op. cit.*, p.90.

69. *ibid*, p.158.

70. Friedrich Nietzsche, *The Antichrist, op. cit.*, p.166.

71. Friedrich Nietzsche, *The Will to Power, op. cit.*, pp. 98-99.

72. Friedrich Nietzsche, *The Antichrist, op. cit.*, pp.158-9.

73. George Allen Morgan, *op. cit.*, p.343.

74. Friedrich Nietzsche, *The Antichrist, op. cit.*, p.163.

75. H.S. Chamberlain, *op. cit.*, p.187.

76. *ibid*, p.189.

77. Gerald Suster, *op. cit.*, p.111.

78. *ibid*, p.111.

CHAPTER THREE

1. Friedrich Nietzsche, *The Will to Power, op. cit.*, p. 148.

2. Friedrich Nietzsche, *Thus Spoke Zarathustra, op. cit.*, p. 137.

3. Nietzsche, in George Allen Morgan, *What Nietzsche Means, op. cit.*, p.118.

4. Gerald Suster, *Hitler Black Magician, op. cit.*, p.60.

5. Friedrich Nietzsche, *Thus Spoke Zarathustra, op. cit.*, p. 137.

6. George Morgan, *What Nietzsche Means*, op. cit., p. 59.

7. Walter Kaufmann, *Nietzsche: Philosopher, Psychologist, Antichrist, op. cit.*, p.346.

8. Friedrich Nietzsche, *Thus Spoke Zarathustra, op. cit.*, p.59.

9. Friedrich Nietzsche, *Ecce Homo* (London: Penguin Books, 1992), p.103.

10. Nietzsche, *The Will to Power, op. cit.*, pp.376-7.

11. Albert Chandler, *Rosenberg's Nazi Myth*, op. cit., p.78.

12. Friedrich Nietzsche, *Thus Spoke Zarathustra*, op. cit., pp. 274-5.

13. Friedrich Nietzsche, *Twilight of the Idols, op. cit.*, p.65.

14. Albert Chandler, *Rosenberg's Nazi Myth, op. cit.*, pp.66-67.

15. Friedrich Nietzsche, *Thus Spoke Zarathustra, op. cit.*, p.111.

16. *ibid.*, p.218.

17. Friedrich Nietzsche, *The Will to Power, op. cit.*, p.4.

18. *ibid*, p.17.

19. Friedrich Nietzsche, *Thus Spoke Zarathustra, op. cit.*, p.139.

20. Nietzsche, the Will to Power, quoted in Keith Ansell-Pearson, *An Introduction to Nietzsche as Political Thinker* (Cambridge: Cambridge University Press, 1994), p.122.

21. Friedrich Nietzsche, *Thus Spoke Zarathustra, op. cit.*, p.219.

22. Friedrich Nietzsche, *The Will to Power, op. cit.*, p.413.

23. Friedrich Nietzsche, *Human, All-Too-Human* (Cambridge: Cambridge University Press, 1986), p.12-13.

24. This passage was taken from the work of Louis Pauwels & Jacques Bergier, *The Morning of the Magicians,* op. cit., p.179, whose chapter on Nazism has a very suggestive title: *"A Few Years in the Absolute Elsewhere"*.

25. George Morgan, *What Nietzsche Means, op. cit.*, p. 324.

26. Friedrich Nietzsche, *The Will to Power, op. cit.*, p.321.

27. Friedrich Nietzsche, *Thus Spoke Zarathustra, op. cit.*, p. 42.

28. Malcom Quinn, *The Swastika: Constructing the Symbol* (London: Routledge, 1994), pp. 133-4.

29. Friedrich Nietzsche, *On the Genealogy of Morals* (New York: Russel & Russel Inc., 1964), p.167.

30. Nietzsche, quoted in Bruce Detwiler, *Nietzsche and the Politics of Aristocratic Radicalism, op. cit.*, p.78.

31. Friedrich Nietzsche, *The Will to Power, op. cit.*, p. 375.

32. Friedrich Nietzsche, *Thus Spoke Zarathustra, op. cit.*, p. 138.

33. Pauwels & Bergier, *op. cit.*, p. 209.

34. Friedrich Nietzsche, quoted in William T. Bluhm, *Theories of the Political System: Classics of Political Thought and Modern Political Analysis* (New Jersey: Prentice Hall, 1978), p.486.

35. Adolf Hitler, *Mein Kampf, op.cit.*, pp.407-8.

36. Friedrich Nietzsche, *The Will to Power, op. cit.*, pp.549-550.

37. Friedrich Nietzsche, *Thus Spoke Zarathustra, op. cit.*, p.45.

38. Friedrich Nietzsche, *Beyond Good and Evil* (London: Penguin Books, 1990), p. 61.

39. Adolf Hitler, *Mein Kampf, op. cit.*, p.399.

40. Friedrich Nietzsche, *The Will to Power, op. cit.*, p. 189.

41. *ibid.*, p.75.

42. Friedrich Nietzsche, *Beyond Good and Evil*, op. cit., p.158.

43. Albert Chandler, *Rosenberg's Nazi Myth, op. cit.*, p. 7.

44. *ibid.*, p.92.

45. Leslie Paul Thiele, *Friedrich Nietzsche and the Politics of the Soul* (New Jersey: Princeton University Press, 1990), p.211.

46. Friedrich Nietzsche, *Thus Spoke Zarathustra, op. cit.*, p.212.

47. Friedrich Nietzsche, *Beyond Good and Evil*, op. cit., p.194.

48. *ibid*, 196.

49. Friedrich Nietzsche, *The Will to Power, op. cit.*, p. 530.

50. Friedrich Nietzsche, *Beyond Good and Evil*, op. cit., pp. 195-6.

51. Friedrich Nietzsche, *The Will to Power, op. cit.*, pp.496-7.

52. Nietzsche, quoted in Bruce Detwiler, *op. cit.*, p.135.

53. John Keegan, *Waffen SS: The Asphalt Soldiers* (New York: Ballantine Books, 1970), pp. 13-14.

54. Friedrich Nietzsche, *Beyond Good and Evil*, op. cit., p. 197.

55. Friedrich Nietzsche, *On the Genealogy of Morals, op. cit.*, p. 54.

56. Friedrich Nietzsche, *Thus Spoke Zarathustra, op. cit.*, p.93.

57. Friedrich Nietzsche, *Ecce Homo, op. cit.*, p. 98.

58. *ibid*, p. 100.

59. Friedrich Nietzsche, *Human All Too Human*, p. 7.

60. Friedrich Nietzsche, *Beyond Good and Evil*, op. cit., p.97.

61. Friedrich Nietzsche, *Thus Spoke Zarathustra, op. cit.*, p. 299.

62. Friedrich Nietzsche, *On the Genealogy of Morals, op. cit.*, p.103.

63. Albert Chandler, *Rosenberg's Nazi Myth, op. cit.*, p.74.

64. Friedrich Nietzsche, *Beyond Good and Evil*, op. cit., p.104.

65. Friedrich Nietzsche, *Thus Spoke Zarathustra, op. cit.*, p. 297.

66. *ibid*, p.86.

67. *ibid*, 41.

68. *ibid*, 110.

69. *ibid*, pp. 109, 110, 112.

70. *ibid*,. 138.

71. Friedrich Nietzsche, *The Will to Power, op. cit.*, p. 513.

72. George Morgan, *op. cit.*, p.36.

73. Friedrich Nietzsche, *The Will to Power, op. cit.* p. 519.

74. Adolf Hitler, *op. cit.*, p. 290.

75. Gerald Suster, *op. cit.*, p. 140.

76. Karl Loewith, *From Hegel to Nietzsche* (London: Constable, 1965), p. 187.

77. Nicholas Goodrick-Clarcke, *op. cit.*, p. 157.

78. *ibid*, p. 157.

79. Nietzsche, quoted in Walter Kaufmann, *op. cit.*, p. 370.

80. Friedrich Nietzsche, *Thus Spoke Zarathustra, op. cit.*, p. 174.

81. *ibid*, pp.44, 90, 91.

82. Gerald Suster, *op. cit.*, p. 85.

83. Adolf Hitler, *op. cit.*, p. 298.

84. Nicholas Goodrick-Clarcke, *op. cit.*, p. 157.

85. Adolf Hitler, *op. cit.*, p. 297.

86. Friedrich Nietzsche, *Beyond Good and Evil*, op. cit., pp. 194.

87. William L. Shirer, *The Rise and Fall of the Third Reich* (New York, Simon and Schuster, 1960), p. 100.

88. Pauwels & Bergier, *op. cit.,*, p. 210.

89. Friedrich Nietzsche, *Thus Spoke Zarathustra, op. cit.*, p. 74.

90. Crane Brinton, *Nietzsche* (Cambridge: Harvard University Press, 1941), pp. 212-3.

91. William Shirer, *op. cit.*, p. 86.

92. Eberhard Jaeckel, *Hitler's Worldview: A Blueprint for Power* (Cambridge: Harvard University Press, 1981), p. 96.

93. Gerald Suster, *op. cit.*, p. 143.

94. John Keegan, *op. cit.*, p. 18.

95. Friedrich Nietzsche, *Thus Spoke Zarathustra, op. cit.*, p. 75.

96. *ibid*, p. 74.

97. *ibid, p.* 74.

98. *ibid*, p. 75.

99. Friedrich Nietzsche, The Will to Power, *op. cit.*, pp. 525-6.

100. Eberhard Jaeckel, *Hitler's worldview, op. cit.*, p. 93.

101. William Shirer, *op. cit.*, p. 86.

102. Friedrich Nietzsche, *Early Greek Philosophy* (New York: Russel & Russel, 1964), p. 7.

103. Adolf Hitler, *op. cit.*, p. 294.

104. Friedrich Nietzsche, *Thus Spoke Zarathustra, op. cit.*, p. 231.

105. Friedrich Nietzsche, *On the Genealogy of Morals, op. cit.*, p. 161.

106. Friedrich Nietzsche, *Beyond Good and Evil, op. cit.*, p. 159.

107. Gerald Suster, *op. cit.*, p. 184.

108. J.S. Conway, *The Nazi Persecution of the Churches 1933-45* (New York: Basic Books, Inc., 1968), p. 152.

109. Friedrich Nietzsche, The Will to Power, *op. cit.*, p.467.

110. *ibid*, p. 458.

111. *ibid*, p. 518.

112. *ibid*, p.471.

113. Friedrich Nietzsche, *On the Genealogy of Morals, op. cit.*, p. 91.

114. Ofelia Schutte, *Beyond Nihilism: Nietzsche Without Masks* (Chicago: University of Chicago Press, 1984), pp. 156-7.

115. Friedrich Nietzsche, *Thus Spoke Zarathustra, op. cit.*, pp.71-2.

116. Bruce Detwiler, *op. cit.*, p. 193.

117. William Shirer, *op. cit.*, p. 937.

118. Heinrich Himmler, quoted in Gerald Suster, *op. cit.*, p. 159.

119. Pauwels & Bergier, *op. cit.*, p. 204.

120. Arthur Danto, *Nietzsche as Philosopher* (New York: The MacMillan Company, 1965), p. 158.

121. Adolf Hitler, *op. cit.*, p. 295.

CHAPTER FOUR

1. Friedrich Nietzsche, *Thus Spoke Zarathustra*, op. cit., p. 143.

2. Friedrich Nietzsche, *Beyond Good and Evil*, op. cit., p. 67.

3. Friedrich Nietzsche, *Early Greek Philosophy- The Greek State* (New York: Russel & Russel Inc, 1964), p. 14.

4. Friedrich Nietzsche, *The Will to Power*, op. cit., p. 111.

5.Nietzsche, quoted in Bruce Detwiler, *Nietzsche and the Politics of Aristocratic Radiclism*, op. cit., p. 129.

6. Friedrich Nietzsche, *Beyond Good and Evil*, op. cit., pp. 125, 127.

7. Friedrich Nietzsche, *The Will to Power*, op. cit., p. 397.

8. Friedrich Nietzsche, *Human, All-too-Human*, quoted in Crane Brinton, *Nietzsche*, op. cit., p. 125.

9. Adolf Hitler, *Mein Kampf*, op. cit., p. 78.

10. Friedrich Nietzsche, *The Will to Power*, op. cit., p. 77.

11. Friedrich Nietzsche, *Beyond Good and Evil*, op. cit., p. 127.

12. Friedrich Nietzsche, *The Antichrist*, op. cit., p. 191.

13. Friedrich Nietzsche, *The Will to Power*, op. cit., p. 32.

14. Friedrich Nietzsche, *The Will to Power*, op. cit., p. 32.

15. Adolf Hitler, *Mein Kampf*, op. cit., p. 65.

16. Friedrich Nietzsche, *Early Greek Philosophy- The Greek State*, op. cit., p. 7.

17. Friedrich Nietzsche, *The Will to Power*, op. cit., p. 126.

18. Friedrich Nietzsche, Beyond Good and Evil, quoted in Bruce Detwiler, *Nietzsche and the Politics of Aristocratic Radicalism*, op. cit., p. 152.

19. Friedrich Nietzsche, *The Will to Power*, op. cit., p. 462..

20. Friedrich Nietzsche, *Thus Spoke Zarathustra*, op. cit., p. 229.

21. Friedrich Nietzsche, *Early Greek Philosophy- The Greek State*, op. cit., p. 15.

22. Barbara Miller & Leila J. Rupp (trans.), *Nazi Ideology Before 1933* (Austin & London: University of Texas Press, 1978), p. 100.

23. Friedrich Nietzsche, *Beyond Good and Evil*, op. cit., p. 173.

24. Friedrich Nietzsche, *Beyond Good and Evil*, op. cit., p.121.

25. Adolf Hitler, *Mein Kampf,* op. cit., p. 81.

26. Friedrich Nietzsche, *The Will to Power*, op. cit., p. 397.

27. Keith Ansell-Pearson, *An Introduction to Nietzsche as Political Thinker* (Cambridge: Cambridge University Press, 1994), p. 150.

28. Friedrich Nietzsche, *Thus Spoke Zarathustra*, op. cit., p. 89.

29. Friedrich Nietzsche, quoted in Bruce Detwiler, *Nietzsche and the Politics of Aristocratic Radicalism,* op. cit., p. 96.

30. Friedrich Nietzsche, *Beyond Good and Evil*, op. cit., p. 72.

31. Friedrich Nietzsche, *Thus Spoke Zarathustra,Early Greek Philosophy-The Greek State*, op. cit., p. 7.

32. Friedrich Nietzsche, *Thus Spoke Zarathustra*, op. cit., p. 282.

33. Friedrich Nietzsche, *The Will to Power*, op. cit., p. 33.

34. Friedrich Nietzsche, *Ecce Homo* (London: Penguin Books, 1979-1992), p. 99.

35. Friedrich Nietzsche, *Thus Spoke Zarathustra*, op. cit,. p. 46.

36. Friedrich Nietzsche, *Thus Spoke Zarathustra*, op. cit, p. 220.

37. Friedrich Nietzsche, *Thus Spoke Zarathustra*, op. cit, p. 298.

38. A term used by Georg Brandes, the renowed Danish scholar, to describe Nietzsche's philosophy- Nietzsche was delighted with it, saying it best expressed his political opinions.

39. Friedrich Nietzsche, *The Will to Power*, op. cit., p.457.

40. George Morgan, *What Nietzsche Means*, op. cit., p. 368.

41. Friedrich Nietzsche, *The Will to Power*, op. cit., p. 493.

42. Friedrich Nietzsche, *Beyond Good and Evil*, op. cit., p. 192.

43. Friedrich Nietzsche, *The Antichrist*, op. cit., pp. 188-9.

44. Gerald Suster, *Hitler Black Magician* (London: Skoob Books Ltd., 1996), p.171.

45. Friedrich Nietzsche, *Twilight of the Idols*, op. cit., p. 113.

46. Friedrich Nietzsche, *Thus Spoke Zarathustra*, op. cit, p. 124.

47. Gerald Suster, op. cit., p. 171.

48. Barbara Miller & Leila J. Rupp (trans.), *Nazi Ideology Before 1933*, op. cit., p. 101.

49..Adolf Hitler, op. cit., p. 429.

50. Friedrich Nietzsche, *Thus Spoke Zarathustra*. op. cit., p. 220.

51. Herbert F. Ziegler, *Nazi Germany's New Aristocracy; The SS Leadership, 1925-1939* (New Jersey: Princeton University Press, 1989), p. 37.

52. Friedrich Nietzsche, *Thus Spoke Zarathustra*, op. cit., pp. 220-1. Nietzsche also said: *"Aristocrats so far, spiritual and temporal, prove nothing against necessity for a new aristocracy"* (*The Will to Power*, p. 500).

53. Friedrich Nietzsche, *Thus Spoke Zarathustra*. op. cit., pp. 227, 259.

54. George Mosse, *Nazi culture*, op. cit., p. 105.

55. Herbert F. Ziegler, *Nazi Germany's New Aristocracy;* op. cit., p. 58.

56. Herbert F. Ziegler, *Nazi Germany's New Aristocracy;* op. cit., p. 52.

57. Friedrich Nietzsche, *The Will to Power*, op. cit., p. 495-496.

58. Friedrich Nietzsche, *Beyond Good and Evil*, op. cit., p. 192.

59. Friedrich Nietzsche, *The Will to Power*, op. cit., p.497.

60. *ibid*, pp. 495-6.

61. *ibid*, p. 478.

62. *ibid*, p. 47.

63. Herbert F. Ziegler, *Nazi Germany's New Aristocracy;* op. cit., p. 53.

64. Friedrich Nietzsche, *Beyond Good and Evil*, op. cit., p. 192.

65. Ofelia Schutte, *Beyond Nihilism: Nietzsche Without Masks* (Chicago: University of Chicago Press, 1984), p. 163.

66. Mark Warren, *Nietzsche and Political Thought* (Cambridge: The MIP, 1988), p. 240.

67. Frank H. Hankins, *The Racial Basis of Civilisation*; A Critique of the Nordic Doctrine (New York & London: Alfred A. Knopf), p. 293.

68. Adolf Hitler, op. cit., p. 293.

69. Friedrich Nietzsche, *The Will to Power*, op. cit., p. 517.

70. Friedrich Nietzsche, *Thus Spoke Zarathustr*a. op. cit., p. 103.

71. Friedrich Nietzsche, *The Will to Power*, op. cit., p. 410.

72. Friedrich Nietzsche, *On the Genealogy of Morals*, op. cit., p. 169.

73. Quoted in Mark Warren, *Nietzsche and Political Thought*, op. cit., p. 241.

74. Frank H. Hankins, *The Racial Basis of Civilisation*; A Critique of the Nordic Doctrine, op. cit., p. 28.

75. *ibid*, p. 39.

76. H.S. Chamberlain, *Foundations of the Nineteenth Century*, op. cit., p. lxv.

77. Adolf Hitler, op. cit., p. 383.

78. Frank H. Hankins, *The Racial Basis of Civilisation*; A Critique of the Nordic Doctrine, op. cit., p. 131.

79. ibid, p. 119.

80. William Ripley, *Races of Europe: A Sociological Study* (New York: D. Appleton & co., 1899) p. 467.

81. Frank H. Hankins, op. cit., p. 132.

82. Helena Petrovna Blavatsky, *The Secret Doctrine* (Los Angeles: The Theosophical Company, 1982), p. 522.

83. Friedrich Nietzsche, *On the Genealogy of Morals*, op. cit., pp. 25-26.

84. Friedrich Nietzsche, *Twilight of the Idols*, op. cit., p. 71.

85. Crane Brinton, *Nietzsche*, op. cit., p.99.

86. Friedrich Nietzsche, *The Will to Power*, op. cit., p. 92.

87. ibid, p. 93.

88. Friedrich Nietzsche, *The Antichrist*, op. cit., p. 187.

89. Friedrich Nietzsche, *Twilight of the Idols*, op. cit., p. 69.

90. Friedrich Nietzsche, *The Will to Power*, op. cit., p. 97.

91. ibid, p. 92.

92. When Nietzsche speaks of the "superior" aristocrats as "the powerful", "the lords", "the commanders", "the possessors", he goes on to specify "that is the meaning of Arya", thus equating the Aryans with the "Masters" (Nietzsche, *On the Genealogy of Morals*, p. 24).

93. Nietzsche recognised *"at the core of these aristocratic races the beast of prey; the magnificent blond brute, avidly rampant for spoil and victory... the beast must get loose again, must return into the wilderness -the Roman,*

Arabic, German, and Japanese nobility, the Homeric heroes, the Scandinavian Vikings, are all alike in this need" (*The Genealogy of Morals*, p. 40).

94. Friedrich Nietzsche, *The Will to Power,* op. cit., p. 93.

95. Nietzsche, *The Will to Power,* quoted in Walter Kaufmann, *Nietzsche: Philosopher, Psychologist, Antichrist,* op. cit., p. 302.

96. Friedrich Nietzsche, *On the Genealogy of Morals,* op. cit., p.26.

97. By "blond beast", Nietzsche means the lion, i.e. the strongest and noblest animal: *"for higher, stronger, more victorious, more joyful men, such as are square-built in body and soul: laughing lions must come!"* (*Thus Spoke Zarathustra*, p. 294).Yet "blond beast" is also a racial term designating a higher race, an aristocratic race: thus did Nietzsche recognise *"at the core of these aristocratic races the beast of prey"* (*Genealogy of Morals*, p. 40), whom Nietzsche called *"my beautiful new race"* (*Thus Spoke Zarathustra*, p. 294).

98. Friedrich Nietzsche, *Twilight of the Idols,* op. cit., p. 67.

99. Friedrich Nietzsche, *On the Genealogy of Morals,* op. cit., p. 41.

100. ibid, p. 25.

101. ibid, p. 76.

102. Hans Guenther, quoted in George Mosse, *Nazi Culture,* op. cit., pp. 64-65.

103. Friedrich Nietzsche, *The Antichrist,* op. cit., p. 180.

104. Adolf Hitler, op. cit., p. 402.

105. Richard Noll, *The Jung Cult- Origins of a Charismatic Movement* (New Jersey: Princeton University Press, 1994), p. 296.

106. George Mosse, *Nazi Culture,* op. cit, p. 58.

107. Friedrich Nietzsche, *The Will to Power,* op. cit., p. 271.

108. ibid, p. 348.

109. ibid, p. 358.

110. ibid, p. 47.

111. ibid, p. 344.

112. Deputy Party Leader Rudolf Hess say, at a mass meeting in 1934: *"National Socialism is applied biology"* (quoted in Robert Jay Lifton, *The Nazi doctors; Medical Killing and the Psychology of Genocide* (New York: Basic Books, 1986), p. 31.

113. Frank H. Hankins, *The Racial Basis of Civilisation*; A Critique of the Nordic Doctrine, op. cit., p. 35.

114. Albert Chandler, *Rosenberg's Nazi Myth*, *op. cit.*, p. 70.

115. H.S. Chamberlain, *Foundations of the Nineteenth Century*, op. cit., p. 519.

116. ibid, p. 77.

117. Louis Pauwels & Jacques Bergier, *The Morning of the Magicians* (New York: Stein and Day, 1963), p. 178.

118. Friedrich Nietzsche, *Beyond Good and Evil*, op. cit., p. 152.

119. Friedrich Nietzsche, *The Will to Power*, op. cit., p. 519.

120. Friedrich Nietzsche, *Thus Spoke Zarathustra*, op. cit, p. 100.

121. Adolf Hitler, quoted in William Bluhm, *Theories of the Political System*, op. cit., p. 495.

122. Adolf Hitler, op. cit, 383.

123. Gerald Suster, op. cit., p. 166.

124. Friedrich Nietzsche, *The Will to Power*, op. cit., p. 534.

125. ibid, p. 501.

126. ibid, p. 471.

127. Friedrich Nietzsche, *Beyond Good and Evil*, op. cit, p. 126.

128. Adolf Hitler, op. cit., 562.

129. Herbert F. Ziegler, *Nazi Germany's New Aristocracy*, op. cit., p. 52.

130. Friedrich Nietzsche, *The Will to Power*, op. cit., p. 388.

131. Friedrich Nietzsche, *Thus Spoke Zarathustra*, op. cit., pp. 92, 95.

132. Robert Jay Lifton, *The Nazi doctors*, op. cit., p. 43.

133. Rick Wilford, *Fascism*, in *Political Ideologies: An Introduction* (London & New York: Routledge, 1994), p. 203.

134. Robert Jay Lifton, *The Nazi doctors*, op. cit., p. 17.

135. Friedrich Nietzsche, *Thus Spoke Zarathustra*, op. cit., p. 95.

136. Friedrich Nietzsche, in *Twilight of the Idols*, quoted in Bruce Detwiler, *Nietzsche and the Politics of Aristocratic Radicalism*, op. cit., p. 108.

137. Adolf Hitler, op. cit., p. 402.

138. Hitler, quoted in Robert Jay Lifton, *The Nazi doctors*, op. cit., p. 22.

139. Ofelia Schutte, *Beyond Nihilism: Nietzsche Without Masks* (Chicago: University of Chicago Press, 1984), pp. 157.

140. Bruce Detwiler, *op. cit.*, p. 193.

141. Friedrich Nietzsch, *Beyond Good and Evil*, op. cit., p. 121.

142. ibid, p. 137.

143. Friedrich Nietzsche, *On the Genealogy of Morals*, op. cit., p. 169.

144. Friedrich Nietzsch, *Beyond Good and Evil,* op. cit., p. 152.

145. Friedrich Nietzsche, *Human, All-Too-Human,* op. cit., p. 149.

146. Friedrich Nietzsche, *On the Genealogy of Morals,* op. cit, pp. 25-26.

147. Hitler, quoted in William Shirer, *The Rise and Fall of the Third Reich,* op. cit., p. 88.

148. Adolf Hitler, op. cit., p. 286.

149. ibid, 286.

150. Friedrich Nietzsche, *Thus Spoke Zarathustr*a, op. cit., pp. 75, 76.

151. ibid, pp. 77-78.

152. Friedrich Nietzsche, *Twilight of the Idols,* op. cit., p. 74.

153. Keith Ansell-Pearson, *An Introduction to Nietzsche as Political Thinker,* op. cit., pp. 74- 75.

154. Friedrich Nietzsche, *Twilight of the Idols,* op. cit., p. 105.

155. Friedrich Nietzsche, *The Will to Power,* op. cit., pp. 395-6.

156. Adolf Hitler, op. cit., p. 386.

157. Bruce Detwiler, op. cit, p. 61.

158. Friedrich Nietzsche, *Early Greek Philosophy- The Greek state,* op. cit., p. 13.

159. Friedrich Nietzsche, *On the Genealogy of Morals,* op. cit, p. 103.

160. Friedrich Nietzsche, *The Will to Power,* op. cit., p. 382.

161. ibid, p. 386.

162. Robert Jay Lifton, *The Nazi doctors,* op. cit., p. 17.

163. Adolf Hitler, op. cit., pp. 391,393, 394.

164. Nietzsche, quoted in Keith Ansell Pearson, op. cit., p. 148.

165 . Friedrich Nietzsche, *The Will to Power*, op. cit., p. 504.

166. ibid, p. 519.

167. Friedrich Nietzsche, *Thus Spoke Zarathustra*, op. cit., p. 168.

168. ibid,, pp. 227, 259.

169. ibid, p. 42.

170. Friedrich Nietzsche, *The Will to Power*, op. cit., p. 465.

171. ibid, p. 479.

172. Friedrich Nietzsche, *Ecce Homo*, op. cit, p. 97.

173. Bruce Detwiler, op. cit., p. 56.

174. H.S. Chamberlain, op. cit., p. 542.

175. Adolf Hitler, op. cit., p. 396.

176. Friedrich Nietzsche, *The Will to Power*, op. cit., p. 503.

177. Friedrich Nietzsche, *Thus Spoke Zarathustra*, op. cit., p. 221.

178. Hitler, quoted in William Bluhm, *Theories of the Political System*, op. cit., pp. 493-4.

179. Hitler, quoted in Gerald Suster, op. cit., p. 132.

180. *"Nationality has no foundation in race"*: William Ripley, *Races of Europe: A Sociological Study*, op. cit., p. 15.

181. Adolf Hitler, op. cit, p. 312.

182. H.S. Chamberlain, op. cit., p. 529.

183. ibid, pp. 371-372.

184. Raphael Patai (ed.), *The Republic of Lebanon* (substractor's monograph) New Haven: Printed by Human Relations Area File, 1956), p. 86.

185. *"supra-national Aryan state"*: Nicholas Goodrick-Clarcke, The Occult Roots of Nazism, op. cit., p. 104.

186. Robert Jay Lifton, *The Nazi doctors*, op. cit., p. 14.

187. Crane Brinton, *Nietzsche*, op. cit., p. 221.

188. Friedrich Nietzsche, *Twilight of the Idols*, op. cit., p. 72.

189. Crane Brinton, op. cit., pp 114-115.

190. Friedrich Nietzsche, *Twilight of the Idols*, op. cit., p. 71.

191. Friedrich Nietzsche, *On the Genealogy of Morals*, op. cit, p. 41.

192. ibid, p. 26.

193. Adolf Hitler, op. cit., pp. 395-396.

CHAPTER FIVE

1. Albert Chandler, *Rosenberg's Nazi Myth*, op. cit., p. 30.

2. Friedrich Nietzsche, *The Antichrist*, op. cit., p. 146.

3. Albert Chandler, Rosenberg's Nazi Myth, op. cit., p. 100.

4. Adolf Hitler, *Mein Kampf,* op. cit., p. 305.

5. H.S. Chamberlain. quoted in Frank H. Hankins, *The Racial Basis of Civilisation*; A Critique of the Nordic Doctrine, op. cit., p. 82.

6. ibid, p. 81.

7. Albert Chandler, *Rosenberg's Nazi Myth*, op. cit., p. 30.

8. William T. Bluhm, *Theories of the Political System: Classics of Political Thought and Modern Political Analysis* (New Jersey: Prentice Hall, 1978), p. 494.

9. Albert Chandler, *Rosenberg's Nazi Myth*, op. cit., p. 30.

10. *"The Jewish instinct of the 'chosen': they claim all the virtues for themselves without further ado, and count the rest of the world their opposites; a profound sign of a vulgar soul"*: Friedrich Nietzsche, *The Will to Power*, op. cit., p. 116.

11. Friedrich Nietzsche, *The Will to Power*, op. cit., p. 117.

12. Friedrich Nietzsche, *Thus Spoke Zarathustra*, op. cit., p. 258.

13. ibid, p. 260.

14. Crane Brinton, *Nietzsche*, op. cit., p. 215.

15. *"perhaps the young stock-exchange Jew is the most disgusting invention of mankind"*: Friedrich Nietzsche, *The Will to Power*, op. cit., p. 290.

16. Friedrich Nietzsche, *On the Genealogy of Morals*, op. cit., p. 56.

17. Hitler, quoted in Eberhard Jaeckel, *Hitler's Worldview: A Blueprint for Power* (Cambridge: Harvard University Press, 1981), p. 101

18. Adolf Hitler, *Mein Kampf*, op. cit., p. 325.

19. ibid, p. 65.

20. ibid, p. 320.

21. ibid, p. 325.

22. Friedrich Nietzsche, *On the Genealogy of Morals*, op. cit, p. 33.

23. Friedrich Nietzsche, *Beyond Good and Evil*, op. cit., p. 118.

24. Friedrich Nietzsche, *The Antichrist*, op. cit., p. 171.

25. ibid, p. 169.

26. Friedrich Nietzsche, *Twilight of the Idols*, op. cit., p. 69.

27. Friedrich Nietzsche, *The Antichrist*, op. cit., p. 193.

28. ibid, p. 166.

29. Friedrich Nietzsche, *The Will to Power*, op. cit., p. 101.

30. Friedrich Nietzsche, *The Antichrist*, op. cit., p. 175.

31. Robert Jay Lifton, The Nazi Doctors: Medical Killing and the Psychology of Genocide (New York: Basic Books, 1986), p. 478.

32. Adolf Hitler, *Mein Kampf,* op. cit., p. 312.

33. Friedrich Hertz, *Race and Civilization* (London: Kegan Paul, Trench, Trubner & co., Ltd, 1928), p.206.

34. ibid, p. 276.

35. Adolf Hitler, *Mein Kampf,* op. cit., p. 305.

36. Friedrich Nietzsche, *The Will to Power*, op. cit., p.117.

37. ibid, p. 111.

38. Adolf Hitler, *Mein Kampf,* op. cit., p. 326.

39. Friedrich Nietzsche, *The Antichrist,* op. cit., p. 146.

40. Adolf Hitler, *Mein Kampf,* op. cit., pp. 302-3.

41. Friedrich Nietzsche, *The Antichrist,* op. cit., pp. 146-7.

42. ibid, p. 147.

43. Friedrich Nietzsche, *On the Genealogy of Morals*, op. cit, p. 31.

44. Friedrich Nietzsche, *Beyond Good and Evil*, p. 118.

45. Friedrich Nietzsche, *On the Genealogy of Morals*, op. cit, pp. 30-1.

46. ibid, pp. 54-55.

47. ibid, pp. 54-55.

48. ibid, pp. 32-33.

49. Bruce Detwiler, *Nietzsche and the Politics of Aristocratic Radicalism*, op. cit., p. 120.

50. Louis Pauwels & Jacques Bergier, *The Morning of the Magicians*, op. cit., pp. 178-9.

51. Adolf Hitler, *Mein Kampf*, op. cit., p. 65.

CHAPTER SIX

1. Friedrich Nietzsche, *Thus Spoke Zarathustra*, op. cit., p. 253.

2. Crane Brinton, quoted in Bruce Detwiler, *Nietzsche and the Politics of Aristocratic Radicalism*, op. cit., p. 2.

3. Alfred Bauemler, quoted in Crane Brinton, *Nietzsche*, op. cit., p. 209.

BIBLIOGRAPHY

Ansell- Pearson, Keith, *An Introduction to Nietzsche as Political Thinker* (Cambridge: Cambridge University Press, 1994).

Blavatsky, Helena Petrovna, *The Secret Doctrine* (Los Angeles: The Theosophical Company, 1982).

Bluhm, William T., *Theories of the Political System: Classics of Political Thought and Modern Political Analysis* (New Jersey: Prentice Hall, 1978).

Brinton, Crane, *Nietzsche* (Cambridge, Massachusetts: Harvard University Press, 1941).

Chamberlain, Houston Stewart, *Foundations of the Nineteenth Century* (London: John Lane The Bodley Head, 1912).

Chandler, Albert, *Rosenberg's Nazi Myth* (New York: Greenwood Press, 1968).

Conway, J.S., *The Nazi Persecution of the Churches 1933-45* (New York: Basic Books, Inc., 1968).

Danto, Arthur, *Nietzsche as Philosopher* (New York: The MacMillan Company, 1965).

Detwiler, Bruce, *Nietzsche and the Politics of Aristocratic Radicalism* (Chicago and London: The University of Chicago Press, 1990).

Goodrick-Clarcke, Nicholas, *The Occult Roots of Nazism- Secret Aryan Cults and their Influence on Nazi Ideology* (London, New York: I.B. Tauris & Co. Ltd., 1992).

Hankins, Frank H., *The Racial Basis of Civilization- A Critique of the Nordic Doctrine* (New York & London: Alfred .A. Knopf, 1926).

Herz, Friedrich, *Race and Civilization* (London: Kegan Paul, Trench, Trubner & co., Ltd, 1928).

Hitler, Adolf, *Mein Kampf* (Boston: Houghton Mifflin Company, 1971).

Howard, Michael, *The Occult Conspiracy- Secret Societies: Their Influence and Power in World History* (Rochester, Vermont: Destiny Books, 1989).

Jaeckel, Eberhard, *Hitler's Worldview: A Blueprint for Power* (Cambridge: Harvard University Press, 1981).

Jung, Carl Gustav, *Nietzsche's Zarathustra* (New Jersey: Princeton University Press, 1988).

Jung, Carl Gustav, *The Psychology of Nazism* (New Jersey: Princeton University Press, 1989).

Kaufmann, Walter, *Nietzsche: Philosopher, Psychologist, Antichrist* (New Jersey: Princeton University Press, 1974).

Keegan, John, *Waffen SS: The Asphalt Soldiers* (New York: Ballantine Books, 1970).

Lifton, Jay, *The Nazi doctors; Medical Killing and the Psychology of Genocide* (New York: Basic Books, 1986).

Loewith, Karl, *From Hegel to Nietzsche* (London: Constable, 1965).

Miller, Barbara & Leila J. Rupp (trans.), *Nazi Ideology Before 1933* (Austin & London: University of Texas Press, 1978).

Morgan, George Allen, *What Nietzsche Means* (New York: Harper Torchbooks, 1944).

Mosse, George L., *Nazi Culture- Intellectual, Cultural and Social Life in the Third Reich* (New York: Grosset & Dunlap, 1966).

Nietzsche, Friedrich, *The Antichrist* (London: Penguin Books, 1990).

Nietzsche, Friedrich, *Beyond Good and Evil* (London: Penguin Books, 1990).

Nietzsche, Friedrich, *The Birth of Tragedy* (New York: Russel & Russel Inc., 1964).

Nietzsche, Friedrich, *Early Greek Philosophy* (New York: Russel & Russel, 1964).

Nietzsche, Friedrich, *Ecce Homo* (London: Penguin Books, 1992).

Nietzsche, Friedrich, *Human, All-Too-Human* (Cambridge: Cambridge University Press, 1986).

Nietzsche, Friedrich, *On the Genealogy of Morals* (New York: Russel & Russel Inc., 1964).

Nietzsche, Friedrich, *Thus Spoke Zarathustra* (London: Penguin Books, 1969).

Nietzsche, Friedrich, *Twilight of the Idols* (London: Penguin Books, 1990).

Nietzsche, Friedrich, *The Will to Power* (New York: Random House, 1967).

Noll, Richard, *The Jung Cult- Origins of a Charismatic Movement* (New Jersey: Princeton University Press, 1994).

Patai, Raphael (ed.), *The Republic of Lebanon* (substractor's monograph) (New Haven: Printed by Human Relations Area File, 1956).

Pauwels, Louis & Jacques Bergier, *The Morning of the Magicians* (New York: Stein and Day, 1963).

Peterson, James M., *The Enchanted Alphabet- A Guide to Authentic Rune Magic and Divination* (England: The Aquarian Press, 1988).

Quinn, Malcom, *The Swastika: Constructing the Symbol* (London: Routledge, 1994).

Ripley, William, *Races of Europe: A Sociological Study* (New York: D. Appleton & co., 1899).

Schutte, Ofelia, *Beyond Nihilism: Nietzsche Without Masks* (Chicago: University of Chicago Press, 1984).

Shirer, William L., *The Rise and Fall of the Third Reich* (New York, Simon and Schuster, 1960).

Suster, Gerald, *Hitler Black Magician* (London: Skoob Books Ltd, 1996).

Thiele, Leslie Paul, *Friedrich Nietzsche and the Politics of the Soul* (New Jersey: Princeton University Press, 1990).

Warren, Mark, *Nietzsche and Political Thought* (Cambridge: The MIP, 1988).

Wilford, Rick, *Fascism*, in *Political Ideologies: An Introduction* (London & New York: Routledge, 1994).

Ziegler, Herbert, *Nazi Germany's New Aristocracy- The SS Leadership, 1925-1939* (New Jersey: Princeton University Press, 1989).

ABOUT THE AUTHOR

Abir Taha, currently a diplomat and a "doctorante" in philosophy at the Sorbonne University, is an expert in Nietzschean thought. For years she has extensively read, studied, and analysed Nietzsche's philosophy. She has written several studies and dissertations on philosophy and political theory, particularly Nietzschean thought.

Whereas most Nietzsche scholars ignore the spiritual dimension of Nietzsche's philosophy, the author contends that there lies the essence of the great German philosopher's work. She thus put special focus on Nietzsche's spirituality, which is deeply influenced by Greek and Indian philosophy.

Having deep knowledge of Western and Eastern esoteric thought and the influence of esoteric schools on current political ideologies, the author underwent extensive research on Nazism and its occult roots, paying special attention to Nietzsche's influence on what she calls "Esoteric Nazism", thus unveiling the Nazi Secret Doctrine and establishing a clear link between Nietzsche's philosophy and Nazism as a spiritual Weltanschauung.

The author is currently publishing a book in French entitled "Nietzsche's Coming God, or the Redemption of the Divine".